First-Rate Reading™ Basics

Fluency
Grades 1-3

by Starin W. Lewis

Carson-Dellosa Publishing Company, Inc. • Greensboro, North Carolina

Credits and Dedication

Project Director:

Kelly Gunzenhauser

Layout Design:

Jon Nawrocik

Inside Illustrations:

Stefano Giorgi

Cover Design:

Peggy Jackson

Cover Illustrations:

Stefano Giorgi

This book is dedicated to my friends and family.
Thank you for encouraging me to follow my dreams.
Your support has been overwhelming.

-S. L.

Table of Contents

Introduction

Unlike pre-readers and beginning readers at the kindergarten level, many students in first grade and higher are beginning to grasp the basics of reading, namely phonemic awareness and phonics, as well as other skills such as left-to-right tracking, print awareness, etc. Although some students are just learning to read and are unable to put any additional focus into the task, many students are now able to read with specific purposes. For example, a student who has mastered reading the words in a simple book can now focus on reading that book aloud for different reasons: to be more expressive, to read accurately, to perform the book for an audience, to sound natural and smooth, or to read automatically without sounding out any words. Since readers in grades 1–3 can usually tell the difference between these skills, *First-Rate Reading*™ *Basics: Fluency* activities are sorted into chapters according to which single skill they most specifically address. In the Performance chapter (page 66), students can demonstrate their abilities in all of the skills simultaneously.

Utilize the reproducible Parent Letter (page 4) to help reinforce fluency instruction at home. The more parents read to children, the more fluent their children will become. The Parent Letter helps inform parents about which skills they impart to their children while reading aloud and also offers suggestions for making read-aloud experiences even more valuable to young readers.

Finally, use the Assessment (page 5) to look at students' fluency levels at any time during the school year, including before instruction begins. Assessing students early in the year will help you determine in which areas they need practice. It will also help you group students by skill level, if that is your preference.

Name _____

Parent Letter

Dear Parents/Family:

Research shows that good readers are more successful in school. Reading is used in all other subjects and is critical for success in real life. It is important for your child to develop a solid reading base that extends beyond phonics into other areas such as fluency. Following are suggestions and information about helping your child become a more fluent reader.

Fluency is the ability to read aloud accurately and quickly. If a reader struggles to sound out words or reads in a choppy, very slow, or unnatural way, he will not understand what he is reading as well as he could. Help your child improve his or her fluency by doing the following:

- Read aloud to your child often. Young children need to learn what fluent readers sound like. When you read aloud, read in a clear, strong voice. Read the way you speak if you are talking. Be expressive: if a character is happy, read with a happy voice. Be sure your reading is smooth, fluid, and flowing—not choppy or like a robot. Try changing your voice for different characters. You might feel silly, but your child will absolutely love this!
- Use your finger to track the print (underline words) as you read. This will help your child understand that words and sentences go together and your voice follows the text's patterns. Occasionally, have your child track the print with his or her finger.
- Echo read with your child by having your child repeat the reading after you. Your child will automatically read the text just as you do, including expression, speed, etc. When echo reading, read in short sentences or phrases so that your child can keep up. Track the print so that your child will follow the words with his or her eyes while repeating them.
- Choral read with your child (read at the same time). This works well with simple text, rhyming text, or books your child has nearly memorized. Simply tell your child to join in whenever he or she wants to.

Using these ideas will help your child begin to enjoy reading. For more information, please feel free to contact me.

Sincerely,

_____

Use the following assessment at the beginning of the school year or during each reading unit to identify student needs. Or, administer it as an ongoing tool to assess student progress. A method of assessing each fluency skill is listed below.

Accuracy

To assess for accuracy, provide three books that are grade-level appropriate: one at a low reading level, one at grade level, and one for advanced readers. Make three copies of the Assessment reproducible (page 6). In the space provided or on a separate piece of paper, type a portion of each text (60 words for first grade, 100 words for second grade, 115 words for third grade). Leave space between each line to make brief notes. Make one master copy of each assessment for students to read from and make an additional copy of each appropriate assessment for each student. You will score students on the additional copies as they read from the master copies. Give each student a master copy of the appropriate text. On the corresponding copy of the reproducible, write the student's name and the date, and circle the text level (L=low, A=average, H=high). Then, give the student the master copy of the text to read. Record the start time, then signal the student to begin reading aloud. Follow along on your copy as the student reads. Circle each mistake and write any incorrect words above the correct words. Make two slash marks (//) if the student pauses for more than a few seconds to sound out a word. After the student is finished reading, record the time it took her to read the passage.

To calculate the student's accuracy, write the total number of words in the passage and subtract the number of errors. Then, divide the resulting number of words read correctly by the total number of words in the passage. This will give you a percentage. Students should aim for an accuracy rate of 90% or higher.

Automaticity

To evaluate automaticity, compare the time each student takes to read the passage aloud to grade-level norms. For example, by the end of first grade, students should be able to read a 60-word passage in one minute. Less time is better than average; more time is below average. However, make sure that you don't encourage students to "speed read" without expression and comprehension. Here are grade-level norms:

- End of first grade—a passage of 60 words should take one minute.
- End of second grade—a passage of 90–100 words should take one minute.
- End of third grade—a passage of 115 words should take one minute.

(Source: *Put Reading First: The Research Building Blocks for Teaching Children to Read*, U.S. Department of Education, 2001, p. 29)

Expressiveness, Naturalness, Smoothness, and Flow

These skills are more subjective. For expressiveness, rate the student from one (lowest) to five (highest) on how well he expresses emotion, changes voices for characters, paces himself correctly for the content, and sounds animated. Write any additional comments on his expressiveness below the numbers.

For naturalness, smoothness, and flow, rate the student from one (lowest) to five (highest) on how smoothly he reads and on how conversational his reading sounds. Add any comments about the student's smoothness on the lines below.

Finally, add any other thoughts, concerns, or celebrations in the space at the end of the assessment.

Name _____

Date _____

Assessment

Text Level (circle one): L   A   H

Type passage here:

Accuracy: _____ _____ _____

# of total words – # of errors = # of words correct

_____ _____ _____

# of words correct ÷ # of total words = accuracy rate

Automaticity: _____ _____ _____

start time   end time   total time

Expressiveness (circle one):   1   2   3   4   5

_____

Naturalness, Smoothness, and Flow (circle one):   1   2   3   4   5

_____

Additional Comments: _____

_____

_____

First-Rate Reading™: Fluency • CD-104016 • © Carson-Dellosa
Basics

Accuracy

Introduction

Consider the many different components of teaching fluency. Of course, a fluent reader needs to be quick, but a fast reader who makes several errors along the way is not an effective reader. The purpose of reading is to comprehend what is being read. Therefore, a key component of reading fluency is accuracy. Students need to read most of the words correctly in order to understand what they are reading. The word *accuracy* comes from the Latin word *accurare*, which means "to do with care." As you teach fluency, guide students to read with care.

Why Is Accuracy Important?

In the introductory lesson, help students understand why it is important to be accurate. Select a book that students have heard before. Look through the book and choose a few pages on which to make reading mistakes. Write four or five comprehension questions related to those mistakes on small pieces of paper. For example, you may purposely mispronounce the main character's name throughout the reading. One of the comprehension questions could be: *What is the main character's name?* If you read the wrong words in any important part of the plot, one question could be: *What is the main idea of the story?* Before reading the story, give each question to a student. Read the story and remember to make mistakes throughout. Then, have students ask you the comprehension questions. As you try to answer them, make it clear to students that you are having a hard time understanding the story. Afterwards, ask, "Why do you think it's important to read all of the words correctly?" Students should know that it is so that the story is understood. Emphasize that accuracy, or reading the words correctly, really does affect comprehension.

Catch the Mistake

Set the scene by saying, "Sometimes mistakes just fly out of my mouth!" Give each student a small, foam cup and a sharpened pencil. Help each student push his pencil through the side of the cup near the top. The result should look like a butterfly net. Allow students to practice "catching mistakes" in the air by waving their "nets." Next, choose a familiar book and explain that as you read it, you may make mistakes, such as saying the wrong word or mispronouncing words. Students must listen well, and when they hear a mistake, swoop their "nets" to catch it. After reading, say that it is important for them to catch their own mistakes. If they read words that make no sense and keep reading, they haven't caught their mistakes. Have each student read easy text to a partner and wave the "net" if she catches herself making mistakes. Partners should confirm whether the readers caught the mistakes. Then, let partners reverse roles.

You Be the Judge

Ahead of time, plan for an adult volunteer to read a passage twice to students. Bring in an old trophy, medal, or blue ribbon, or draw a blue ribbon on construction paper and cut it out. Announce that students will be judges in a contest. Explain that you and an invited guest will read the same passage, and students will determine which reading is better. The winner will get the award. Ask your invited guest to read the passage without any mistakes. Allow the guest to go first. Next, read the same passage but make several errors. Make sure the errors are boring and not funny—stumble over words, use incorrect tense or plurals, etc. Ask students which reading was better and why. Guide students to answer that it was easier to understand the reading that had no mistakes. Point out that listening to reading is more enjoyable when there are fewer mistakes.

Circling the Mistakes

Tell students that a great way to make fewer mistakes is to practice, practice, practice. The more they reread a passage, the more accurate they will become. Provide some simple books. Ask each student to select a book and find a paragraph in which she can read all but four or five words. Have the student rewrite the paragraph on a piece of paper, leaving a blank line between each line of text. Direct each student to read the paragraph to herself. As students read, tell them to keep track of the words they missed or stumbled over by circling them with pencils. (Model this a few times, first.) When students are finished, encourage them to ask you, classmates, or volunteers to help them pronounce the difficult words. Next, have students reread the passages. This time, have them circle any difficult words with purple crayons. Hopefully, there will be fewer mistakes. Again, have students ask for help with the difficult words. Tell students to reread the paragraphs a third time and circle the difficult words with orange crayons. Are there fewer circles? For the fourth reading, direct students to circle the difficult words with red crayons. Ask students if they have fewer red circles than pencil circles. Discuss how practicing made reading accurately easier.

Let Me Introduce Myself

This is a great activity for the beginning of the year, but it will work anytime. Give each student a piece of paper and a pencil. Write the following sentence starters on the board: *My name is _____, I have _____ brothers and _____ sisters, My favorite game is _____, My favorite food is _____, The best time I ever had was _____.* Tell students to copy the sentences and fill in the blanks. Then, have students mingle, find partners, and read their introductions. Each partner should listen and hold up a finger for every mistake and mispronounced word. When students have finished reading, tell the partners to reveal the number of mistakes and identify them if possible. Have the partners switch roles. Repeat the process for a total of five introductions. Ask students if they made fewer mistakes by the fifth introduction. Emphasize that the more they reread text, the more accurate they will become.

Bull's-Eye

Ahead of time, make a class set of the Bull's-Eye reproducible (page 10). Select text that is about 100 words in length and that is either slightly difficult for the student or at her independent read-aloud level. Make five copies of the text for each student and staple four of them on top of the Bull's-Eye reproducible, leaving one loose for the student. Give each student a packet and ask her to number the copies of the text 1–4. Announce that each student will read the text aloud to you or to an adult volunteer. The goal is to be as accurate as possible while reading at a normal rate. Tell students that they will get a chance to reread the texts a few times. During center time or independent reading time, listen to individual students read from the extra copy and circle each word missed on the first copy from the packet. Review the results, and give the correct pronunciation of each missed word and its meaning, if necessary. Then, turn to the copy of the Bull's-Eye reproducible. Mark the number of words the student missed on the bull's-eye, and date the mark. (If the student missed more than 20, make a mark outside the bull's-eye.) Encourage each student to practice until he hits the bull's-eye (makes no mistakes). Allow the student to take the packet and extra copy back to his seat and reread the passage as you work with another student. Schedule time over a few weeks to listen to students reread their passages. Continue to mark their progress on the remaining copies of the reproducible and praise improvements.

Looking for Clues

Tell students that they can look for clues in words to read them more accurately. The letters in the word will help them recognize the word and say it correctly. Write the following words on the board: *bamboozle, divulge, gargoyle, inference, jovial, marsupial, nebula, omnivore, quota, random,* and *ultraviolet.* Say a word correctly and have students search for clues to identify where the word is on the board. To help them as they search for clues, encourage each student to make an *O* with his hands to look like a detective's magnifying glass. Remind students to think about the sounds of the letters and words, and how they may or may not match the written words. When students find the word on the board, have them raise their hands. Call on a student to use her "magnifying glass" to touch the word on the board and allow her to explain what clues she used to find the word.

Bull's-Eye

Read the text. Mark the number of mistakes you made. Date the mark. Try to hit the bull's-eye!

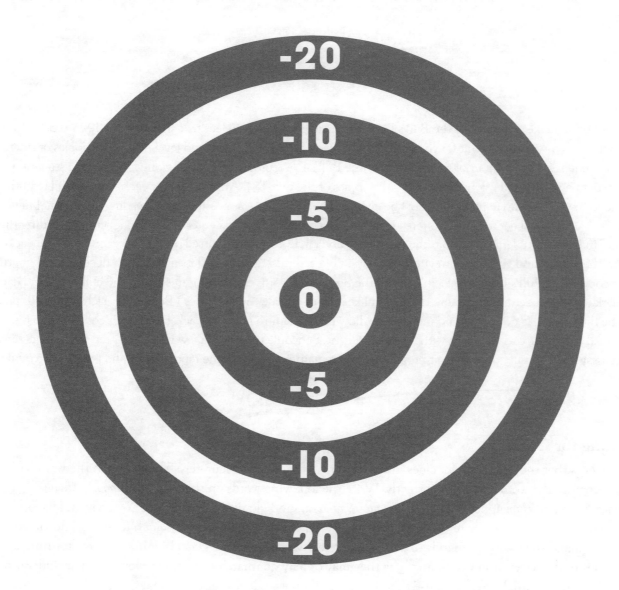

First-Rate Reading™: Fluency • CD-104016 • © Carson-Dellosa
Basics

Most Mispronounced Words

On the Pronunciation Flash Cards reproducible (page 12), fill in the blank cards with words that students repeatedly mispronounce, then give a copy to each student. Explain that these are frequently mispronounced words. Review each word by saying it, having students repeat it, and then using the word in a sentence. Ask students to make suggestions for remembering how to say the words. Next, provide sentence strips for students. Tell each student to cut out five words of her choice from the worksheet. On sentence strips, have her write sentences using the words but leaving blank spaces for the words. Instruct her to glue the word cards to the appropriate blank spaces on the sentence strips. Let students practice reading their sentences. Assign small groups and let members read their sentences to each other. When the reading is finished, display the sentences on a bulletin board titled "Can You Pronounce These Words?"

Accuracy Game

Tell students that realizing when they have made mistakes is a key to improving accuracy. Some readers say nonsense words and keep reading even though the words do not make sense. Emphasize that good readers are aware of what is and is not correct. Play an accuracy game. Put two, two-partner teams together to create a group of four students. Give each group one copy of the Accuracy Game reproducible (page 13). Tell the groups to cut apart the sentences and place them facedown on the floor or table. Explain that each sentence contains a mistake. Have one member of each team choose a sentence and practice reading it, including the mistake. If a reader is unsure of how to read the sentence, he may ask a member of the other team for help, but away from his partner. He should then read the sentence to his partner, who must listen closely and find the error. If the partner identifies the mistake, his team gets one point. If the partner does not find the mistake, his team gets no points, and the other team may try to correct the sentence for a point. The team member who chose the sentence must identify the mistake and say the sentence correctly. Then, it is the other team's turn. Let students track points by making tally marks on a piece of paper. The game ends when all sentences have been read. The team with the most points wins.

Peer Running Record

Encourage students to help each other read accurately. Have each student select a slightly challenging passage of about 50 words. (Slightly challenging means that a student should not find more than five difficult words when skimming.) Have each student rewrite the passage on a piece of paper, leaving a blank line between each line of text. Make a copy of each student's passage. Allow students to practice reading their passages aloud four times. Pair students and explain how to keep a running record. One student should read her passage while her partner follows along on his copy and circles misread words and incorrect pauses or expression for punctuation. Remind students that they should be supportive, helpful listeners. At the end of the reading, the partner should write the number of mistakes at the top of the page. Then, have partners switch roles. Tell students that if they missed more than five words, they should practice their accuracy. If they missed fewer than five words, they can move to more difficult passages.

11

Pronunciation Flash Cards

Cut apart the words. Practice saying them
correctly, then make sentences with five of the words.

ask	because	clothes
escape	February	from
height	library	spaghetti
were	where	

First-Rate Reading™: Fluency • CD-104016 • © Carson-Dellosa
Basics

Name _____

Accuracy Game

Cut apart the sentences. Decide which team goes first. Choose a sentence from the strips and read it to your partner. If your partner can find the mistake, give your team a point.

I have only one dogs.

This gift was form my mom.

When I go camping, I ride houses.

I walk to school wet my friends.

My dad sad that I was smart.

I lick to play soccer during recess.

I carry my books in my packback.

I like to eat paper for lunch.

Cut!

Encourage a little directing with this activity. Tell each student to select a short poem (approximately 50–100 words). Give each student a piece of white construction paper. Tell him to cut about 1" (2.5 cm) off the longer side of the paper, then attach the corner of the paper strip to the rest of the paper with a paper fastener. It should look like a clapboard (the black-and-white mechanism that is snapped together in front of a movie camera at the beginning of a take to facilitate editing). Assign students to pairs. One student will be the "actor" and the other student will be the "director." Explain that the director will "clap" the top strip of paper (move it up and down) to signal the actor. The actor will read the poem to the director. The director will listen and make a tally mark on the "clapboard" each time the actor stumbles over a word, mispronounces a word, or seems to skip a word. When the actor is finished, the director will say, "Cut!" and will review the actor's mistakes. The actor may have two more "takes." Emphasize that students should not expect to be perfect, just to make fewer mistakes each time. After the actor and director have consulted for a total of three times, have students reverse roles. Remind students that one of the best ways to become more accurate with their reading is to reread passages several times.

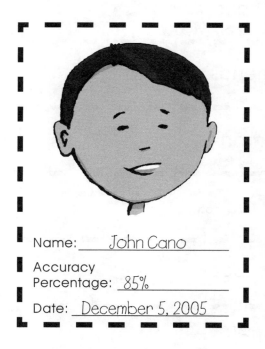

Name: _John Cano_

Accuracy
Percentage: _85%_

Date: _December 5, 2005_

Trading Cards

Explain how important it is for athletes to be accurate. A basketball player needs to throw the ball accurately so that the ball will go in the basket. A baseball player needs to pitch the baseball accurately so that he reaches the strike zone. This accuracy is so important that people keep track of it. Some of the statistics on trading cards are based on the accuracy of the athletes. Give students the opportunity to create their own fluency trading cards. Give each student a copy of the Trading Cards reproducible (page 15). Have each student write his name and draw a self-portrait on each card. Tell students to cut out the cards and staple them together in the corner. For each student, choose a reading passage of about 100 words that is near his independent reading level. Have the student read his passage aloud to you while other students complete independent work. Tally the number of mistakes as you follow along on the student's passage. Calculate the accuracy percentage by dividing the number of correct words by the total number of words in the passage. Write the accuracy percentage and date on the first trading card. Explain to students that the higher the number they receive, the better the accuracy rate. Repeat this procedure five times throughout the school year. Encourage each student to compare the accuracy statistics on his trading cards as he improves.

Trading Cards

Write your name on all six cards. Draw your picture on all six cards. Color and cut apart the cards. Use them to help you and your teacher track your reading accuracy rate.

Name: _____

Accuracy
Percentage: _____

Date: _____

Name: _____

Accuracy
Percentage: _____

Date: _____

Name: _____

Accuracy
Percentage: _____

Date: _____

Name: _____

Accuracy
Percentage: _____

Date: _____

Name: _____

Accuracy
Percentage: _____

Date: _____

Name: _____

Accuracy
Percentage: _____

Date: _____

Accuracy in Reporting

State that it is important for reporters to be accurate when reading the news. If they make mistakes, they make false information public. For example, read the following sentence as if you were a reporter: "Thirty students passed their end-of-year tests at _____ Elementary School." Reread the sentence, changing the number from thirty to three hundred. Ask students how people hearing the first (incorrect) information might feel about the school! Let students be reporters. Have students write their own news stories about school events. Have each student practice reading the first paragraph in his story aloud at least four times. Remind students to make sure their readings are accurate. Schedule time for their "news reports." Throughout the day, have students read their paragraphs to the class as you review them for accuracy. Compliment journalists and correct reports as needed.

Sticky Review

Ahead of time, record yourself reading a short book. Make several mistakes as you read the book. At the end of the reading, tell students where the mistakes were (note the page numbers) and correct the mistakes—all while you record. Place the tape and book at a listening center, along with several sticky notes. Explain that some people are blind and cannot read books printed with ink. People who can see can volunteer to record themselves reading books aloud so that blind people can listen to the books. To make sure that the reading is accurate, an editor listens to each tape before a blind person receives it. Assign students to be sound editors at a listening center. Explain that they will visit the center and listen to a tape that has mistakes. Their job as editors is to follow along with the book, listen to the tape, and note any mistakes by placing sticky notes on the pages next to the places in the text where the mistakes occur. Tell students that at the end of the tape, the mistakes will be reviewed. Remind students that it is important for them to monitor their own reading so that they can correct their own errors, as well.

Show-and-Tell

Turn students' love of Show-and-Tell into a motivator for accuracy. Tell students to think of items from home that they wish to bring in to share. Then, have each student write a brief description of the item, including interesting details. Possible topics include the object's name, its history (where it came from, the story behind it), and why he wanted to show it and tell about it. Direct students to practice reading their Show-and-Tell descriptions at least four times. When students can read their descriptions without any errors, allow them to bring in their items. Check student readiness by having each student read his description to you. If it is error-free, schedule a time for the student to present. If the student makes mistakes, suggest that he practice some more. Allow students to read to you until they make no mistakes so that everyone gets to bring in an item. Students may also want to write about additional items once everyone has had a turn at Show-and-Tell.

Cooking Class

Bring crackers, peanut butter, plastic knives, and raisins for the class to make a snack. (Before completing any food activity, get families' permission and check for food allergies and religious or other preferences.) Hold a pretend cooking class. Encourage students to put on their imaginary chefs' hats and aprons. Read the following recipe while students pretend to cook it.

- First, take out a cracker.
- Use a plastic knife to spread a bunch of pasta on it.
- Next add rats' tails. Make a smiley face out of the rats' tails. Enjoy!

Ask students if they think that would be a good snack. What do they think went wrong? (Students will probably shout that you read the recipe incorrectly!) Reveal to students that you did make some mistakes in your reading. Practice rereading the recipe several times, then tell the class you will try again. Say,

- "First take out a cracker—that was correct." (Give each student a cracker.)
- "Use a plastic knife to spread a bit of peanut butter, not pasta, on the cracker." (Give students peanut butter and plastic knives.)
- "Next add raisins—not rats' tails." (Provide raisins for students.)
- "Make a smiley face out of the raisins. Enjoy!"

Ask, "How important was it that I was an accurate reader?" Allow students to eat their snacks.

How-To Project

Emphasize the importance of accuracy in directions. Plan a quick lesson on how to make something easy, such as paper airplanes. Make a model paper airplane first, writing the directions as you make it. Give each student a piece of paper. Read the directions as students fold their airplanes, but make a few significant mistakes while reading. Then, ask students if their paper airplanes look and fly like yours. Ask, "Why is it important to be accurate while reading directions?" Reread the directions correctly and let students fly their airplanes. Next, tell students they are going to teach quick "how-to" lessons that show the audience how to make something. Direct each student to think of something she knows how to make: a picture, a sandwich, a kite, a "cootie catcher" or "fortune teller," or anything that she feels comfortable teaching. Then, have the "teachers" write directions for how to make their objects. Suggest that they create the objects at home while writing so that they do not forget any steps. Have students reread their lessons several times. When the "teachers" are ready, ask families to provide extra supplies, and schedule time for them to teach the class. Spread out the "teaching" over several days to maintain student interest. The test of accuracy will be if their "students'" final projects turn out correctly. Post the projects and directions on a bulletin board.

Hide-and-Seek

Play Fluency Hide-and-Seek. Tell each student to choose a small object to hide, decide where he will hide the object, and then write directions to find it. The directions should start at a specific point and end where the object is hidden. Read this example to students: *Start at the doorway. Walk five steps forward. Turn left. Walk six steps forward. Turn right. Go to the board. Look under the chalk tray. You should find an eraser taped underneath.* Ask students why it is important to be accurate when giving directions. Then, give students time to write their directions, test them, and reread them at least four times. Divide the class into two groups. Tell half of the students to cover their eyes while the rest of the students hide their objects. Pair a "hider" with a "seeker." Tell the hider to read his directions to the seeker. The hider should pause after each step until the seeker is ready for the next step. Accurate readers should be able to lead their partners to the hidden objects. Reverse the roles and repeat.

Books on Tape

Motivate students to improve their accuracy with student-created listening centers. Ahead of time, ask parents to donate audiocassettes that are blank or that can be taped over. First, have each student select a book from the classroom collection that is slightly difficult for her. (Try to provide more than one copy of each book.) Next, have students practice until they can read the books with no errors. Monitor several practices or have an adult volunteer monitor. Then, set up a tape recorder in a quiet area. Train students how to place a cassette in the recorder and press record and stop. Allow students to record themselves reading their stories. Tell students to say "beep" when it is time to turn the page, or provide a bell to ring. Place students' finished tapes and corresponding books at a listening center for classmates or younger students to enjoy.

Pronunciation Guide

Remind students that mispronouncing words affects accuracy. Show students phonetic symbols in a dictionary, and explain that they show readers how to say words and divide words into syllables. Have students create pronunciation guides. Give each student two copies of the Pronunciation Guide reproducible (page 19) and have him select a book with some new words in it. Pair each student with a partner. Have each partner look in her book for four words she can't pronounce and write them on the reproducibles. Instruct partners to exchange the words they choose. Each student's task is to learn to pronounce his partner's words and then think of ways to show his partner how to say them. (If students are not sure how to say words, let them ask you or other students.) On the reproducible, have each student write each word like he would say it, as opposed to the way it is spelled. For example, the word *pronunciation* may look like "pro-nun-see-**ay**-shun." Instruct each student to also write a rhyming word and a sentence using the word. Have students cut apart the reproducibles' sections. Assemble the sections into a class book. Put the words in alphabetical order, glue each word to a page, and add a cover and the title *Class Pronunciation Guide*. Tell students to use the guide when they read words they don't know. Encourage students to add to the guide when they find new words.

Pronunciation Guide

Write your partner's words, then write
the pronunciation. You may include a rhyming word to help with the
pronunciation. Next, write a sentence that includes the word. Write
your partner's name on the bottom lines and cut out each form.

Word: _____

Pronunciation: _____

Rhyming Word: _____

Sentence: _____

_____

_____

_____

Partner's Name: _____

Word: _____

Pronunciation: _____

Rhyming Word: _____

Sentence: _____

_____

_____

_____

Partner's Name: _____

Guest Reader

Give students the opportunity to be guest readers. Ahead of time, ask the media specialist or other teachers if your students could come to the library or their classrooms to read aloud, preferably to younger students. (If this is not possible, students can read to your class.) Direct each student to choose a book. Allow time for students to read their books several times. When they feel they can read their books perfectly, have them read the books to you or to an adult volunteer. If you feel satisfied that each student is capable of reading his book without any errors, schedule time for the student to be a guest reader. Students will be proud to read to a younger grade and show off their accuracy skills!

Reverse Spelling Test

To help students pronounce words correctly, give them a reverse spelling test. On a regular spelling test, the teacher says a word and students try to spell it correctly. This time, you will spell a word and a student will try to say it correctly. First, have a warm-up. Write a list of 10 words that typically give students difficulty while reading. Review the words with students. Then, give each student a pencil and paper. Spell the first word and have students write the word on their papers. Pronounce the word and have students repeat after you. Say a sentence with the word in it and pronounce the word again. Repeat with the other words. Throughout the week, review the words and allow students time to study. At the end of the week, give the reverse spelling test. Pair students. Have each pair decide who the "speaker" is and who the "checker" is. After you spell a word, instruct each speaker to whisper the word in a checker's ear. Then, pronounce the word aloud for students. If a speaker was correct, tell the checker to write the number of the word and a smiley face. If a speaker was incorrect, tell the checker to write only the number of the word. Spell the first five words, then have partners reverse roles. Continue with the last five words, then have partners exchange papers and write their names on them. Tell students that if they missed no words or one word, they were very accurate. If they missed two or more, they need to work to improve their accuracy.

Bedtime Story

Reverse roles by having students read bedtime stories to their families. Instruct each student to select a short story to read aloud at home. Schedule time for students to practice reading their stories aloud four times. When each student can read her story perfectly, have her read it to a partner. If the partner confirms that the reading was error free, send a note and the book home with the student. In the note, explain that the student has been practicing her reading and wishes to read a bedtime story to her family, and leave space for an adult's signature to confirm that the assignment was completed. Encourage families to wear pajamas and enjoy the stories!

Automaticity

Introduction

Fluent readers quickly recognize words in a text and read at an appropriate pace. This skill (automaticity) allows the reader to concentrate on the meaning of the text instead of on decoding the words. The brain is incapable of doing both at the same time. This is why slow, nonfluent readers often lose track of the meaning—they are too focused on keeping up the pace. Automaticity frees the brain, allowing it to comprehend the text. Automaticity is an important part of becoming a fluent reader.

Slow and Unsteady

In order to show students how important automaticity is, prepare to do one of the worst readings of your life. This reading will be the anti-example of automaticity. Select a story that is unfamiliar to students. Gather the class together. Begin reading extremely slowly. Stop several times through the book to sound out words. "Drag out" the text as much as possible. Make it difficult for students to get a sense of what the story is about. When you have finished reading, give each student a copy of the Slow and Unsteady reproducible (page 22). After a few confused looks, ask if anyone is having difficulty answering the questions. Ask, "Why?" Students should answer that the flow of the story was interrupted so many times that they lost the meaning (in student language, of course). Explain that you were giving an example of what a nonfluent reader sounds like. State that one skill of a fluent reader is the ability to recognize words quickly in order to keep the pace moving. The term for this is *automaticity*. Explain that students can understand a story better if their word recognition is automatic. Reread the story aloud, but this time read it at a fluent pace. Give students another chance to answer the questions on the reproducible.

Choral Reading

Ahead of time, select a book with a repetitive chorus, such as *Millions of Cats* by Wanda Ga'g (Putnam, 1997). Use a big book, if possible, or write the chorus on the board. First, guide students as they read the chorus together. Tell the class that the chorus they practiced is repeated throughout the book. Determine a signal to give students, such as pointing to the class, when they should read the chorus together. Practice giving the signal and reading before starting the story. When students are able to read the chorus together, begin the story. After the reading, ask students if they could read the chorus more easily after rereading it several times. Explain that rereading words is a great way to improve automaticity. Students do not have to stop and sound out words by the end because they have practiced so much.

Name _____

Slow and Unsteady

Listen to the story. Answer the questions.

1. What was the main idea of the story?

   _____

   _____

   _____

2. Write the important events of the story in sequence.

   _____

   _____

   _____

3. Name the main character(s). _____

   _____

4. Identify the problem and resolution in the story. _____

   _____

   _____

5. What was the best part? _____

   _____

First-Rate Reading™: Fluency • CD-104016 • © Carson-Dellosa
Basics

Make It Snappy

Tell students that automaticity means to recognize words "just like that." (Use your fingers to snap.) The more words students know automatically, the less they have to stop and decode (sound out the letters to discover the words). The less students stop and decode, the more they understand a text's meaning. Select 10 words from a high-frequency word list to write on the board. Give each student 10 index cards. Direct students to copy each word onto an index card, then practice reading the words quickly. Pair students. Have one student in each pair be the "reader" and the other student be the "snapper." The snapper should show the reader one index card and watch the clock for 10 seconds as the reader tries to read the card. At the end of 10 seconds, the snapper must snap his fingers. If the reader reads the word correctly, the snapper should put the card in the automatic pile. If the reader makes a mistake or cannot read the word quickly enough, the snapper should put the card in the nonautomatic pile. Have students switch roles and work with a different word. After students finish reading the words, they will know which to practice. Schedule time for students to repeat the activity and to notice if they have fewer words in the nonautomatic pile the second time. Later, challenge students to read the words in five seconds, then in two seconds. When students have mastered all 10 words, create a new set of words.

Automatic Robots

Collect tissue boxes (any size) and long cardboard tubes. Explain that robots "know" things automatically because they have been programmed to say things correctly. Have students "program" and build their own robots. Write 10 words on the board that frequently appear in students' reading. Have each student copy each word on an index card. Work with students to pronounce the words correctly, then tell them to build their robots. Distribute the boxes and tubes and art supplies (scissors, markers, construction paper, glue, crayons, etc.). Instruct students to use the supplies to make robots and explain that the only requirement is that the holes in the tissue boxes must be the robots' mouths. On another day, when the robots are complete, pair students. Have partners work together to see if their robots are "programmed correctly." Tell Partner A to read one of Partner B's cards to himself and then show the card to his partner. Partner B should then look at the card, put it in her own robot's mouth (through the hole in the tissue box), and say the word in a robotic voice. If Partner A hears the word he read on the card, the robot was "programmed" correctly. If not, the robot needs to be "reprogrammed." (In other words, the student needs to practice the word.) The partners should then switch roles, alternating between reading and selecting cards. Reward students by putting treats inside the robots' mouths for students to find.

Hopscotch

Use movement to reinforce fluency. Take students to the playground. Assign them to groups of three or four. Give each group a piece of chalk to draw a hopscotch board. Tell students to write a high-frequency word in each square. Suggest a few for them to practice. Then, let the groups play hopscotch. Each student should slide a small rock to the first square, then hop over that square to the next one. Each player must read each word when he hops on it, and must hop to the end and back. On the way back, let the student pick up his rock, hop on the square and read the word, and hop out. Then, it is the next player's turn to slide her rock to the next square. Students should continue to play and work their way to the ends of the hopscotch grids. By hopping several times, students will be rereading the words and practicing automaticity.

Automaticity Buzz

In this game, students get points for recognizing words quickly. Make a list of grade-level, high-frequency words that would help students' automaticity if they recognized them easily. Choose one word for every three students. For each word, write a sentence on a sentence strip and underline the word. Finally, find three "buzzers," such as kazoos or portable, tap-on lights. (Or, have students make buzzing noises.) Give each student a copy of the word list to practice reading several times. Then, let students play Automaticity Buzz. Have students form three lines. Show a sentence strip to the first student in each line. Give these students five seconds to read the sentence silently, recognize the high-frequency word, and sound their "buzzers" when they know the word. The first student to buzz in should say the underlined word. If the student is correct, his team gets a point. If the student is wrong, allow the other two players chances to buzz in, again allotting five seconds. After a student gives the correct answer, the students who are at the fronts of the lines must go to the ends, and the next three players may take their turns. Play until all sentence strips have been read. The team with the most points at the end of the game wins.

Personal Best

Copy the Personal Best reproducible (page 25) for each student. Select a slightly challenging passage for each student to read. Explain that a great way to improve automaticity is to read the same passage several times. During independent reading time, ask each student to read to you. Time the student and track the number of errors by making tally marks on a piece of paper. Write the student's name on the reproducible. Record the date, amount of time it took to read the passage, and the number of errors on one of the stripes. Give the student time to practice. Repeat this process three more times over several days. After four readings, direct each student to look for her personal best—the fastest reading with the fewest errors. Have each student write her personal best in the center of the medal on the reproducible. Celebrate with students when they have improved their automaticity.

First-Rate Reading™: Fluency • CD-104016 • © Carson-Dellosa
Basics

Personal Best

Read a passage four times.
Your teacher will record the
date, your time, and the
number of errors. Find
your personal best!

Date:
Time:
Number of Errors:

Date:
Time:
Number of Errors:

Date:
Number of Errors:
Time:

Date:
Number of Errors:
Time:

_____'s

Personal Best

Date: _____

Time: _____

Beat the Clock

Have students try to "beat the clock" by reading words automatically. Write 12 words for students to practice. Have each student copy the list onto a piece of paper. Review the words. Give students five minutes to practice reading the list, then give each student a copy of the Beat the Clock reproducible (page 27) and have him write his name on it. Assign students to groups of three. Explain that one group member will be the reader, another will be the checker, and the third will be the timer. Allot 30 seconds for the reader to read the words correctly. Have the timer time the reader for 30 seconds. When the reader reads the word, the checker should say, "right" or "wrong." If the reader gets the word right, he should read the next word on the list. If the reader gets the word wrong, he must try again until he reads it correctly. At the end of 30 seconds, the timer should say, "Stop." The reader should then look at how many words he read correctly in 30 seconds, and mark the reproducible by writing the number of correctly read words next to the first clock. For example, if the reader read seven words correctly in 30 seconds, he would write a 7 on the first clock. The group members then switch roles. Allow time for students to make several attempts. Each time a student reads, he should record his time on the reproducible. Students should see that repeated readings help them improve their automaticity.

Automatic Cars

Explain that some cars automatically shift gears to go faster. If students learn to recognize words automatically, they will learn to read faster. Practice automaticity by racing cars. On the board, write several words you would like for students to recognize automatically. Give each student a copy of the Checkered Flag reproducible (page 27). Have him cut out the flag and write his name on the back. Assign students to groups of three and review the words. Give each group six pieces of paper. Tell the groups to fold the papers in half from top to bottom. Direct students to copy the words from the board onto the lower halves of their papers, then stand the papers on the floor like tents with the words facing out. Have each group arrange the tents into an oval to create a "racetrack." Give each student a large, pink eraser to be the race (or "erase") car. In each group, one group member will be the racer, one will be the timer, and one will be the checker. The racer should start at the starting line. (Students may determine where that is.) When the checker waves the flag, the timer should watch the clock while the racer moves her race car to the first word and reads it quickly and correctly. The checker should say "yes" or "no" to indicate if it is correct. If the racer is correct, she may move her car to the next word. If the racer is incorrect, she may try again until she is correct. When the racer drives around the track, have the timer announce how long it took. The racer records the time on the back of her flag. Then, have group members change roles. If possible, let each racer try to get a better time.

Beat the Clock

Try to read a list of 12 words in 30 seconds. Record your time with each reading.

_____ _____ _____
time 1   time 2   time 3

- -

Checkered Flag

Race your car around the track. Read the words as you go. Record your times on the back of this flag.

Auto Cards

Have students play cards to review words they should know automatically. Write additional words in the blank cards on the Auto Cards reproducible (page 29) and give each student a copy of the page. Ask students to read the words and use them in correct sentences. Have students cut apart the cards. Assign pairs to play a card game in which the goal is to make a sentence using four words. Have partners combine their cards. Player A should deal four cards to both players, and then put the remaining cards facedown in a pile. Player A should then turn over the top card. Both players must look at their hands, then Player B must try to form a complete sentence using all four cards in her hand. If she cannot, she may either pick up the discarded word card (the card that was turned over) or draw from the pile, and discard a card from her hand. It is then Player A's turn to try to form a complete sentence using all four words in his hand. If he can't, he may take Player B's discarded card or draw a card from the facedown pile. Play continues until one player can form a complete sentence from the words in her hand. That player should then place the four cards faceup on the floor and read the sentence, then stack the cards to make a book, or set. The student with the most books wins.

Masking Tape Sentences

Students will love the novelty of writing on something other than paper or index cards. Direct students to tear off 10 small pieces of masking tape, each about 2" (5 cm) long. Write three words on the board for students to practice and have them copy each word onto a piece of tape. Review the words, then direct students to write sentences using all three words. On the remaining tape, have each student write additional words that can be added to the sentence, then stick the tape on his desk to build the sentence. For example, if the three words on the board are *present, thought,* and *from,* a possible sentence could be: *I thought the present was from Jim.* A student could write the words *I, the, was,* and *Jim* on the blank pieces of tape. Direct students to walk around and read the various sentences. The repeated exposure to the words in different sentences will help increase automaticity.

Partner Reading

Reading with a partner helps both strong and struggling readers learn new words. Pair struggling and strong readers. Ask each pair to think of a picture book they would like to read the class. Have students bring books from home or the school media center. Then, schedule time for partners to read the books together. They may alternate pages or read chorally, but they must practice until they can read the stories without pausing or sounding out words. Encourage partners to help each other with hard words. When partners can read the stories automatically, allow three pairs to read to the class each day.

Auto Cards

Cut apart the cards. Mix them with your partner's cards. Listen to your teacher tell you how to play a card game to improve reading automaticity.

am	are	ball	best	cat
dog	friend	happy	he	I
is	it	like	me	my
play	she	the	to	with
you				

Commercial Break

Ask students to think about television commercials they have seen and share what the commercials were selling. Write students' answers on the board. Tell students that commercials are usually only 15–30 seconds long. If the ads were longer than that, the audience would change the channel. Also, if an actor in a commercial pauses and mispronounces words, he cannot get the message across. Have students write their own TV commercials. Begin by letting each student choose a product from the list on the board or come up with one of her own. Then, ask students to write paragraphs selling their products. Allot 15 seconds for each commercial. They may want to include the products' names, descriptions, cost, why people should buy the products, and where they can be purchased. After students write the ads, let them practice reading them aloud. Remind students that they need to read the text in 15 seconds or less without making mistakes! Encourage students to time themselves using the second hand on a clock. When students feel confident that they can read their commercials within 15 seconds, schedule time for their "commercial breaks." Throughout the day, transition between other activities by timing students reading their commercials.

Wax Museum

Before beginning this activity, have students preview several wax museum Web sites. Let students create their own wax museum. Tell each student to select someone he admires who is still living, such as a movie star, politician, athlete, author, or scientist. Let students research their choices. In the classroom, give each student white construction paper and crayons to a draw picture of his celebrity. (Since crayons are made from wax, the celebrities will be represented in wax.) Have each student tape or staple another piece of construction paper to the back, leaving a hole to stuff the picture with shredded paper to create a three-dimensional effect. Let the student tape or staple the papers closed and glue a flat button to his picture. Next, have each student write a biography in first person as if the celebrity were speaking. Direct students to practice reading their biographies in voices that their celebrities would use, until they can read their biographies automatically without long pauses and incorrect words. When students feel comfortable reading their paragraphs, invite another class to tour the "wax museum." Post the drawings and station each student near his drawing. Allow guests to walk through the museum to see the celebrities. When they want to hear more about the celebrities, instruct the visitors to push the buttons. At that time, students will read their biographies. Students may have several visitors to their pictures, increasing their automaticity even more. Consider extending this activity for a parents' night.

Automatic Pilot

Explain that an *automatic pilot* is a computer that can take over for a pilot between takeoff and landing. A pilot can program the automatic pilot to fly the plane at a certain altitude and speed, and in a certain direction, for a certain amount of time. Have students program their own automatic pilots— their brains! Give each student a copy of the Automatic Pilot reproducible (page 32). Ask, "If you could fly anywhere in the world, where would it be? Why?" Have students write their responses on the reproducibles, draw themselves in the pilots' seats, and cut out the airplanes. Then, direct students to practice reading their paragraphs until words come automatically; students should not need to stop to sound out words. After giving students several opportunities to practice their responses, schedule "travel time" for them to read their responses aloud. After the readings are finished, attach string or fishing line to the airplanes and hang them around the classroom.

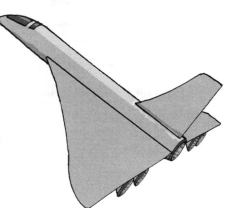

Assembly Line

Repeating words in context will help students recognize words and increase automaticity. Gather students in a circle on the floor. Explain that when a factory builds something, workers can use an assembly line of people who add the same parts to things as they pass by on a conveyor belt. For example, as identical engines pass by, a worker may add a bolt to each engine in the same place. Build a story, assembly-line style. Select a student to write a word to begin the story. For example, if the student chooses *Once*, he should write it on a piece of paper and read it aloud. Next, have the student to the right of the first student choose the next story word and write it on her paper. Then, have the first student read his word again and tell the second student to add her word by reading it aloud. Repeat with remaining students. Continue the story with each student rereading her word after each new word is added. Students may also start new sentences within the assembled story. Continue until all students have added words and the story is finished. Collect the papers and copy the words onto one piece of paper. Let students practice reading the story aloud individually and as a class.

Mingling

Have students socialize with some "new" people. Ask each student to pretend to be any adult—real or imaginary. On the board, write *What is your name? How old are you? Where are you from? What is your occupation?* Have each student write his responses on a piece of paper. Then, have students stand and prepare to "meet" five "new" people. Instruct each student to approach a classmate and ask him the questions from the board. The "new person" should answer by reading her responses. Then, students should switch roles. Repeating the activity and rereading the words will help students with their automaticity. Ask students if their reading got easier the more they responded.

Automatic Pilot

Read the question and write your
response on the lines. Draw a picture of yourself as the
pilot. Cut out the airplane.

If you could fly anywhere in the world, where would it be?
Why? _____
_____
_____

Automated Telling Machines

Explain that automated teller machines (ATMs) dispense cash from adults' bank accounts. Have each student pretend to be a different kind of ATM—an Automated Telling Machine. First, ask, "What would you do with a million dollars?" Have students write their responses on the fronts and backs of large index cards in approximately 50 words and in complete sentences. Allow students to practice reading their complete responses at least four times. They should decode words in the first reading, then practice automaticity in subsequent readings. For each pair of students, provide a sheet of cardboard with a slit cut in it. (Shoe box bottoms or shipping boxes cut into pieces will work.) Have pairs of students sit facing each other with their cards and the cardboard placed on its edge in between them. Direct one student to pick up her partner's ATM card (index card) and slide it through the slit into her partner's hands for him to read. Next, let the partner slide the other card through for the other student to read. After school that day, reward students by leaving play money in the cardboard slits for them to find in the morning.

Hot Potato

Inflate a beach ball and place a strip of masking tape on each colored section. On each strip of tape, write a high-frequency word. Write the same words on the board. Have students sit in a circle to play a variation of Hot Potato. Set a timer for 30 seconds. (Change the number of seconds each time so that students don't know when the buzzer will go off.) Tell students to toss the ball to each other. When a student catches the ball, he should quickly read the word on the tape in the section his right thumb is touching. Right after the student reads the word, tell him whether it is correct. If the student is correct, he should toss the ball to somebody else. If he is incorrect, he should keep the ball until he says the word correctly. When the timer goes off, the student holding the ball is out. When a student is out, he should go to his desk, copy the words from the board, and write a sentence for each word. Repeat with the same list of words or start a new list.

Rate the Reader

To prepare, record yourself reading a story—badly—on audiotape. Make sure there is very little automaticity in your reading by stopping to sound out many words. Acquire or make two more books on tape that have good automaticity. Give each student a copy of the Rate the Reader reproducible (page 34). Play parts of the three stories and have students rate the automaticity of each on a scale of 1–10, with 10 being the best. Begin by playing a good tape. Have students write the title on their reproducibles; listen for long pauses, sounded-out words, and a slow pace; then mark their ratings. Ask students to explain why they chose their answers. Next, play the nonautomatic recording and cue students to rate the story. Again, discuss student ratings and why it is not an automatic piece. End with a good example. After discussing the third book, ask students to summarize what makes a reader an automatic reader or a nonautomatic reader.

Rate the Reader

#1

Write the titles of the books
on the lines. Listen to each story on tape.
Circle numbers to rate each reader's automaticity.
The best score is 10 and the worst score is 1.

Book Title: _____

The reader did not have a lot of long pauses.
1 2 3 4 5 6 7 8 9 10

The reader did not have to decode words.
1 2 3 4 5 6 7 8 9 10

The reader did not read too slowly.
1 2 3 4 5 6 7 8 9 10

Book Title: _____

The reader did not have a lot of long pauses.
1 2 3 4 5 6 7 8 9 10

The reader did not have to decode words.
1 2 3 4 5 6 7 8 9 10

The reader did not read too slowly.
1 2 3 4 5 6 7 8 9 10

Book Title: _____

The reader did not have a lot of long pauses.
1 2 3 4 5 6 7 8 9 10

The reader did not have to decode words.
1 2 3 4 5 6 7 8 9 10

The reader did not read too slowly.
1 2 3 4 5 6 7 8 9 10

First-Rate Reading™: Fluency • CD-104016 • © Carson-Dellosa
Basics

Expressiveness

Introduction

Using an expressive voice is an important part of being a fluent reader. Not only is it more enjoyable to listen to an expressive reader, it also helps with comprehension. Words on a page can be read several different ways. It is when the phrase is read with the proper expression that the true meaning comes through. Explain that an expressive reader does not read in a monotone but matches the emotions the author intended by varying his voice according to the story. The way a person reads a story should be similar to the way a person speaks. Guide students away from monotone reading and toward expressive reading. Help them with such expressive skills as changing voices for different characters, reading in strong voices, and ending questions in a higher tone.

Guess the Emotion

Introduce expressiveness by explaining that there is more to reading than just pronouncing words. Students should use expression when reading aloud or even "in their heads." Give each student a copy of the Guess the Emotion reproducible (page 36). Read the sentence *I want a doughnut!* four different times. Each time, change the emphasis to indicate happy, sad, angry, or excited emotions. For example, when you read the sentence in a happy voice, say the words cheerfully and with anticipation. When you read the sentence in a sad voice, say the words slowly and with a whine. When you read the sentence in an angry voice, add some growls and volume. Finally, when you read the sentence in an excited voice, make your voice high-pitched and a little faster. Each time you read the sentence, have students identify the emotion by circling the corresponding face on the reproducible. Afterwards, emphasize that reading a sentence differently can change its meaning, and it is important to look at the context and punctuation to determine what the author intended.

E is for Expressive

Trace and cut an uppercase letter *E* from construction paper for each student. Explain the difference between reading in a monotone and with expression. When a person reads in a monotone, there is no change in her voice. When a person reads with expression, her tone changes to match characters and punctuation in the story. Read the same sentence once with expression and once in a monotone. Tell students to identify which sentence has expression. Read a short book aloud. Read each sentence twice: once in a monotone, once with expression. After the two readings, ask students to vote whether the first sentence was expressive by holding up their *E*s. If they thought it was monotone, have them keep their *E*s on their desks. Next, ask students to raise their *E*s if they believed the second reading was the expressive one. After reading four or five sentences, ask students how they could tell if a sentence was expressive or monotone. If students find the activity very easy, read a sentence twice in a monotone or twice with expression and see how many students still hold up their *E*s at the correct times.

Guess the Emotion

Listen to each reading.
Circle the matching face.

Reading 1

happy   sad   angry   excited

Reading 2

happy   sad   angry   excited

Reading 3

happy   sad   angry   excited

Reading 4

happy   sad   angry   excited

First-Rate Reading™: Fluency • CD-104016 • © Carson-Dellosa
Basics

Robot Talk

Use a monotone voice to sound like a robot as you ask, "What do you think a robot would sound like if it could talk?" Try some "robot reading" with the class. Have each student choose a favorite book. Assign partners to read one page (approximately 75 words) to each other. In the first reading, have one partner read like a robot while the other partner listens. Then, let the partners switch roles. Next, ask, "What does a person sound like when talking?" Guide students to recognize that a person's speaking voice has different tones and emotions, and that different phrases can be made shorter or longer by altering the speed. Direct students to read the page to each other again, but this time, they should sound like humans. After the second readings, initiate a discussion with the class. Ask, "How were the robot reading and the human reading different?" Tell students that a fluent reader sounds like a human speaking. When students are reading, they should try to sound as natural as possible, not like robots.

Storytelling Tips

Explain that storytellers are very expressive. They read or tell stories with fluency and expression. Tell students that storytellers use some of the following tips for telling a story well. Write the tips listed below on the board. Discuss the meaning of each tip with the class.

Storytelling Tips:

1. Find a story that you really like.
2. Practice reading the story at least four times.
3. Think about how the characters feel.
4. Imagine the characters' different voices and practice them.
5. Read at the same pace as you would speak. Try not to read too fast or too slowly.
6. Avoid long pauses but remember that it is better to pause than to use "filler" words: *um, so, like,* etc.
7. Make sure your voice is loud enough for everyone to hear.
8. Speak clearly.
9. Stand and face your audience. Try not to fidget.
10. Thank your audience.

Assign each tip to a student. (Some tips may be assigned more than once.) Direct each student to write his storytelling tip at the top of a piece of paper. Then, have him illustrate an example of the tip with crayons or markers. Provide each student with a piece of black construction paper on which to center the paper to create a frame. Tell students to glue their papers on top of the construction paper. Display the tips in sequential order in the area where students tell stories.

Using the Tips

Have students review and use the Storytelling Tips activity (page 37) to read stories to the class. Direct each student to choose a short story from the school media center, such as a picture book, folktale, or fable. Allow class time for students to practice reading their stories aloud at least four times. Remind them to use different voices for different characters and to read at the right pace and with expression. Schedule time each day for a few students to read their stories to the class. When each student is finished, have a brief conference with him to talk about which storytelling tips he did well.

Book Festival

Plan a book festival that may last one day or several days. Allow students to be the festival judges. Acquire several books on tape or record yourself reading several books. Have each student listen to two books on tape and rate the expressiveness. Explain that the book with the best score will get a special ribbon. Give each student two copies of the top portion of the Book Festival reproducible (page 39). Review the qualities that students should listen for. When students are ready, play one of the tapes. Afterwards, guide students through the rating sheet. Tell students to rank the book in each category from 1–10. (The worst is 1; the best is 10.) Then, give students another copy of the reproducible, play another book on tape, and have students rate it. Remind students that they are judging the reader's expressiveness, not the content of each book. The book festival may end there, or you may continue this process every day for a week. (Make additional copies of the reproducible as necessary.) At the end of the festival, ask students to turn in their rating sheets. Tally the scores, then announce the winner. Color and cut out the ribbon pattern (page 39) and post it on a bulletin board next to a copy of the winning book cover. Post the other book covers so that students will remember what they read.

Reading Rubric

A rubric is an assessment tool that allows students to rate themselves. It can also serve as a checklist. While students prepare to do a reading, they can look at a rubric to make sure they include necessary components. Review expressive readings from past lessons or read a book expressively. Ask students to think about what makes a reader expressive. Help them recognize that expressive readers change their voice tones, give characters different voices, read at an appropriate pace and volume, and watch for punctuation cues. Write students' answers on the board, then arrange the information into a rating scale of 1–4, with 4 being the best. Use the word *always* when describing a level 4 skill. For example, write *The reader* always *changes her tone of voice.* For levels 3, 2, and 1, use the words *usually, sometimes,* and *never.* Copy the rubric for students, and let them use it as a checklist when they practice and as an assessment tool when they perform.

Name _____

Book Festival

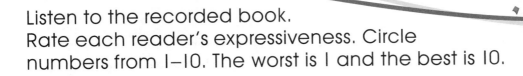

Listen to the recorded book.
Rate each reader's expressiveness. Circle
numbers from 1–10. The worst is 1 and the best is 10.

Book Title: _____

1. The reader's voice changed tone.
   1 2 3 4 5 6 7 8 9 10

2. The reader gave different voices to different characters.
   1 2 3 4 5 6 7 8 9 10

3. The reader's pace was appropriate.
   1 2 3 4 5 6 7 8 9 10

4. The reader's volume was appropriate.
   1 2 3 4 5 6 7 8 9 10

5. The reader made the story fun to listen to.
   1 2 3 4 5 6 7 8 9 10

- - - - - - - - - - - - - - - - - - - -

Winner of the Book Festival

Reading Clues

Explain that there are clues in text that help the reader know how to express words. Give each student a copy of the Reading Clues reproducible (page 41). Review each oval on the reproducible by naming each punctuation mark or type treatment and explaining its purpose as follows.

- For the first oval, tell students that the punctuation is called *quotation marks*. They usually mean that someone is talking. The quotation marks that curve to the right indicate the beginning of dialogue. The quotation marks that curve to the left show the end of dialogue. These marks are a clue to readers that a character is speaking, so a reader may want to change his voice for that character.
- The second oval contains an *exclamation point*. An exclamation point can show anger, happiness, or any other strong emotion. When a sentence ends with an exclamation point, the reader should read the words with more emphasis and maybe with a little more volume.
- The words *ALL CAPS* are written in the third oval. Explain that when words are written in all capital (or uppercase) letters, it usually means to say the words a little louder and with more emphasis than the other words.
- The three dots in a row are called an *ellipsis*. The ellipsis tells the reader that more information is coming or that the speaker was interrupted mid-sentence. If more information is coming, the reader should pause a little. If the speaker was interrupted, the reader may want to change tones or voices and "interrupt himself" as he reads the interrupting words.
- The fifth oval contains a *question mark*. Typically when a person asks a question, the tone in her voice gets higher toward the end of the sentence. Give the example, "May we see a movie today?"

Direct each student to cut out the five ovals on her reproducible. Have students go on a scavenger hunt for these clues. Provide several books for each student. Instruct each student to look through the books to find at least one sentence that shows each clue. When a student finds an example, have him write the sentence, book title, and page number on the back of the corresponding oval. Mix up the ovals and place them in a center along with the books. Let students take turns choosing ovals and looking up the sentences in the books. If a student finds an oval he does not think shows a correct sentence for the clue, instruct him to look it up in the original book to see if it is incorrectly referenced or just incorrectly copied. Place each incorrect oval in an envelope. When each student has looked up some of the sentences, write the incorrect sentences on the board and discuss how each could be changed to correctly use the referenced clue.

Reading Clues

Cut out the ovals. Find the reading clues in stories. Look up an example of each clue, then write it on the back of each oval. Also, write the book title and page number where you found the sentence. Give the completed ovals to your teacher to be used in a center activity.

"Quotation Marks"

1.

Exclamation Point!

2.

ALL CAPS

3.

Ellipsis …

4.

Question Mark?

5.

What's Your Emotion?

Assign students to pairs and put sets of pairs together to form groups of four. Give each group a copy of the What's Your Emotion? reproducible (page 43). Direct students to cut out the cards. Make sure students cut only on dotted lines. Tell students that each pair is a team. Have one person in each group shuffle the cards and place them facedown in a pile. The group should also display the large card that has the emotion words on it. Have each group flip a coin to determine which team is Team A and has the first turn. Instruct Player One from Team A to draw a card from the pile and read the sentence in the emotion he needs to convey. For example, if the card says, *I miss my grandma. sad*, Player One should read the sentence with a sad voice. Player Two from Team A may consult the larger card with the possible emotions listed on it and should guess an emotion. If Player Two guesses correctly, her team gets a point. If Player Two makes an incorrect guess, her team gets no points. The used card goes into a discard pile, and it is then Team B's turn to repeat the procedure described above. When it is Team A's turn again, the two players should switch roles. Point out to students that the more expressive they are when they read the cards, the better their chances for getting points. Play is over when there are no more cards. The team with the most points at the end of the game wins.

Animated Readers

Let students practice using character voices with comic strips. Bring in comics sections from newspapers. Each student will need one comic strip. Tell students that an expressive reader changes his voice for different characters. Give one comic strip to each student. Allow students time to practice reading the comic strips several times. Make sure students understand all of the words as well as the punch lines. Encourage them to imagine what their comic strip characters sound like. After practice time, schedule time for each student to read his comic strip to the class. Create a display by stapling the comic strips to a bulletin board. Add the title "Animated Characters."

What's Your Emotion?

Cut on the dotted lines. Your teacher will tell you how to use the cards for a game.

"My friend hurt my feelings." sad	"I've seen this movie *so* many times." bored	scared
"Pizza is my favorite food." happy	"What is that shadow on my wall?" scared	sad
"I can't believe you cheated!" angry	"I miss my grandma." sad	happy
"There's nothing to do." bored	"My friend is coming over to play today." happy	bored
"I thought I heard something behind the tree." scared	"That's not fair!" angry	angry

A Good Impression

Explain that a good way to learn to read with more expression is to listen to others read. People who provide voices for animated characters make good models for reading expressively because they have to read scripts and create characters from written words, often without the animation having been drawn yet. Tell each student to think of an animated movie or TV character he likes. Have students think about the characters' voices and mannerisms, and prepare them to do impressions of the characters. Give an example by imitating a familiar character to students. When students are ready, have them give their impressions to the class. Encourage the audience to guess who the expressive characters are and talk about how they knew.

Puppet Show

Use puppets to reinforce expression skills. Explain that puppeteers have to be expressive readers. While they are working the puppets, nobody can see their faces, so their voices have to carry the expressions. Put on a class puppet show. Assign students to small groups and let each group choose a fairy tale. Instruct students to choose their roles and practice saying the dialogue as if they are in a play. Schedule time for students to practice reading their lines at least five or six times. Students should not memorize the dialogue. Remind students to imagine what characters sound and act like, and to read with expression. When students have practiced reading, have them make paper bag puppets using lunch bags, paper, markers, crayons, scissors, glue, etc. Turn a long table on its side to make a stage. Have the puppeteers sit behind it and raise the puppets above the table. Direct students to practice synchronizing their reading and puppeteering. When groups are ready, allow them to perform their puppet shows for the class. Consider videotaping the performances, as well as inviting other classes to the shows, too. When the performances are over (and visiting guests have left), make sure to point out good examples of expressiveness from each performance.

Silent Movies

Explain that many years ago, movies did not have sound. Words appeared on a black screen between various scenes of a movie. Let students narrate their own silent movies. Begin by showing an example of a silent movie, if possible. Next, assign students to pairs and tell each pair to choose a short book (or one chapter from a book) that would make a good movie. Explain that in each pair, one person will be the narrator and the other person will be the actor. Direct both students to practice reading the story with expression until they are familiar with it. Remind them that the actor will be a silent actor. He will not be able to express anything with words, so the narrator has to be the expressive reader. When narrators feel ready, have them practice with their actors. Tell the narrators to read the stories while the actors act out the stories silently. Next, direct students to switch roles. Again, allow time for the partners to practice several times. When the partners are ready, encourage them to perform again for the class. Schedule a few "silent movies" a day so that the audience does not get restless.

Radio Time

Tell students that before television was invented, families gathered around radios to listen. The people on radio shows had to read expressively because the audience could not see their faces. Only their words and sound effects could make the shows fun to listen to. Explain that commercials had to be even more interesting because they were very short. Have students perform their own radio commercials. Allow each student to choose a favorite product. (Pair very young or less-skilled students.) Give students time to script brief commercials for their products, including sound effects. Remind students that the reading needs to be accurate, automatic, and expressive. When students are ready, gather the class for story time. Place a radio on top of a desk. Have a student sit next to the table, facing away from students (so that it sounds like the words are coming from the radio). Keep the radio off and have the student read her commercial. Schedule a few commercials each day.

Expression Bingo

Make a copy of the Expression Bingo reproducible (page 46), cut apart the cards, and place them in a bag. Write the words *excited*, *sad*, *happy*, and *angry* on the board. Give each student a copy of the Expression Bingo Grid reproducible (page 47), along with buttons or pennies to use as markers. Next, tell students to write *excited*, *sad*, *happy*, or *angry* in each section in random order. They should use each word four times. To play, reach into the bag and pull out a card. Read it with the emotion listed, then ask each student to place a marker on a square labeled with the corresponding emotion. The first student to get four markers in a row in any direction should say "Bingo!" Reward the winner by letting him read the next sentences.

Expression Bingo

Cut apart the cards. Use them for the Bingo game.

I dropped my ice cream. sad	I can't wait to get our new puppy! excited	I don't like the way you are treating me! angry	I like going to recess. happy
You hurt my feelings. sad	My birthday is today! excited	He broke my new toy! angry	I am glad you are my friend. happy
I can't come to the party. sad	I learned how to swim today! excited	Stop calling me names! angry	I like to eat pizza for lunch. happy
They said I couldn't play with them. sad	We won the game! excited	Stop kicking my chair! angry	Thank you for being so nice. happy

Expression Bingo Grid

Use the grid below to play
Expression Bingo.

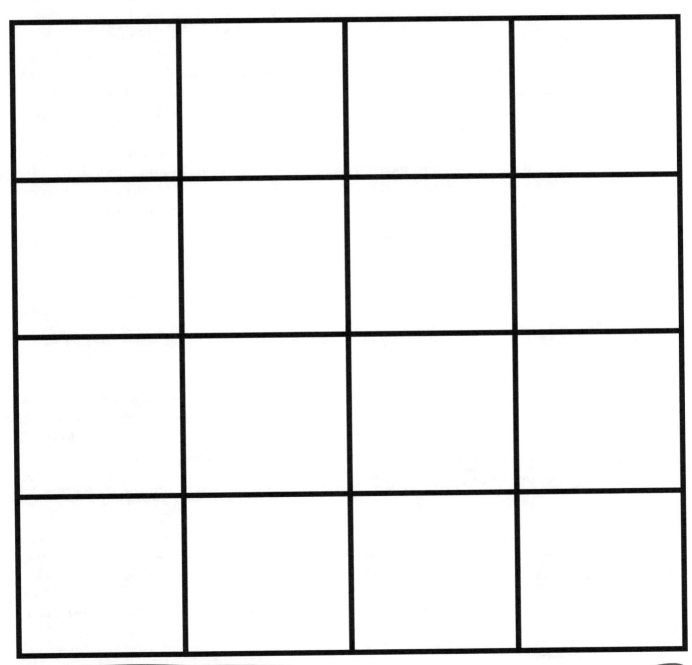

Punctuation Cards

Show students what a difference punctuation makes. Write the following sentence on the board but leave off the end punctuation: *This is my new car.* Next, place a period at the end of the sentence. Explain to the class that a period indicates a statement. There is no excitement; the sentence is stated as a fact. Read the sentence to students as if it were a fact and discuss what the punctuation makes your voice sound like. Next, erase the period and place a question mark at the end of the statement. Tell students that a question mark indicates that the speaker or reader is asking a question. If you put a question mark at the end of this statement, you are questioning whether this is your new car. Explain that the tone of voice goes up when you are asking a question. Read the sentence as a question. Finally, erase the question mark and write an exclamation point at the end of the statement. Tell students that an exclamation point indicates excitement, and by putting an exclamation point at the end of this sentence, you are saying you are excited about getting this new car. Model the excitement by reading the sentence as an exclamation. Give each student three index card halves. Tell students to write a period on one, a question mark on the other, and an exclamation point on the third. Next, have students write the following statements on sentence strips: *She likes cheese on her hamburger; This is my bike; My brother picked up a hairy spider.* Have students use the index card halves instead of writing ending punctuation on the sentence strips. Pair students. Tell students to place the period at the end of the first sentence and practice reading it to their partners with the appropriate expression. Then, have them do the same thing with the question mark and the exclamation point. Tell students to repeat these steps with the remaining two sentences. Review their responses and let volunteers read each sentence with a different punctuation mark.

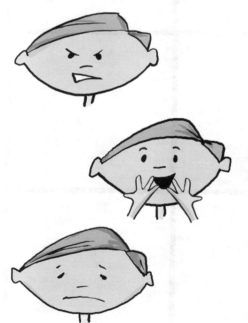

Get the Picture?

Select a book on tape that is new to students and has a very expressive character. (Or, you or an adult volunteer may make a tape.) Give each student two pieces of unlined paper and crayons or markers. Explain that an expressive reader can paint a picture in the audience's mind. Some readers do such a good job of expressing a story that people listening to the story can visualize characters' facial expressions. Ask students to picture the characters' facial expressions as they listen to the tape. At a point in the story at which a character is emphasizing a certain emotion, stop the tape. Tell students to draw a picture of what they think the character's face looks like at that point, with emphasis on the facial expression. Stop the tape again when a character is expressing a different emotion. Again, direct students to draw the character's face. Collect the pictures and tack them to a bulletin board. Read the story from a book, using good expression. Each time you reach a point in the story at which students drew pictures, ask a volunteer to choose a drawing other than her own that shows the character's face at that point in the story.

Most Expressive Reader

Have a contest to see who is the most expressive reader. Make one copy of the Most Expressive Reader reproducible (page 50) for each student. Tell each student to select a short, exciting passage from a favorite book. Allow students to practice reading the passages several times, then have students record their readings. (Ask an adult volunteer to help with the recording, or record each student while the rest of the class is working independently.) Listen to the tapes after school and choose five finalists. Assign each finalist a number to keep the names anonymous. Give each student five ballots (one for each finalist). Tell students to vote for the most expressive reader by rating each reader on a scale of 1–5 for each trait, with 1 being the lowest possible score and 5 the highest possible score. Play all five finalists' readings to the class without revealing their names. After playing the first tape, tell each student to label her ballot *Number 1*, add the rating numbers, and write the total at the bottom. Repeat with additional forms for the other tapes. Collect the ballots and tally the votes. Announce the winner and give the "Most Expressive Reader" a fabulous award, such as extra free reading time.

Nature Show

Capture students' interest with a science twist. Explain that television hosts are often very expressive people. Demonstrate by showing students a few examples of nature shows. Ask students what they think made the hosts expressive. Allow students to perform their own nature shows. Have each student pick a favorite wild animal, then let students conduct research about where the animals live, what they eat, etc. Direct each student to write a paragraph that describes interesting facts about the animal as if he is in the animal's habitat and is watching the animal from up close. Allow time for students to practice reading their paragraphs with expression. If time permits, allow students to provide visual aids, such as drawings of their animals, preprinted pictures, maps showing where the animals live, etc. When students are ready, schedule time throughout the week for them to read their paragraphs to the class.

Name _____

Most Expressive Reader

Use your ballots to vote for the
Most Expressive Reader. Rate each reader on
a separate ballot. Give each reader a score from 1–5
in each area. Add the numbers and write the total at the
bottom of the page.

Reader # __

1. Tone

1   2   3   4   5

reader is monotone   reader changes tone

2. Character Voices

1   2   3   4   5

characters sound the same   characters sound different

3. Pace

1   2   3   4   5

too fast or too slow   just right

4. Volume

1   2   3   4   5

too loud or too soft   just right

5. Fun

1   2   3   4   5

not fun to listen to   very fun to listen to

Total: _____

First-Rate Reading™: Fluency • CD-104016 • © Carson-Dellosa
Basics

Naturalness, Smoothness, & Flow

Introduction

Part of being a fluent reader is reading smoothly. Word-by-word reading makes a passage sound unnatural and choppy. Using phrases rather than word-by-word reading, avoiding "filler" words such as *uh, like, y'know,* etc., and using appropriate pauses between words make text sound natural. Self-awareness of areas for improvement will help students' reading sound effortless, as will repeated practice. For this aspect of fluency, it is also ideal to have students read some of their own writing since it will already be written in a style and vocabulary that is familiar. For this reason, many of the activities in this chapter are writing activities that can be read aloud afterward.

Making Conversation

Recruit a talkative student to model natural conversation. Ahead of time, ask the student if she would feel comfortable talking to you in front of a group. Discuss possible topics (her best birthday, the funniest person she knows, a favorite trip or TV show, etc.) and choose ones that you think will get the most natural responses from this student. Write them on a piece of paper in handwriting the student can read. Ask some fun questions such as, "What can you tell me about your best birthday ever?" and "Who is the funniest person you know?" If her answers are short, try to pry a natural conversation out of her. Then, switch roles and let the student ask you the same questions, but make your responses short, choppy, and unnatural. When the conversation is over, ask the class which responses seemed to flow better. (They should choose the student's responses.) Then, question further to find out why her responses flowed better. Perhaps she spoke in phrases; she didn't stop and say one word at a time. Or, maybe you used a lot of "filler" words. Explain to students that when they read, they should try to make their reading as smooth as conversation. Reading this way makes text more enjoyable to hear and easier to understand.

Put Punctuation Here!

Explain that punctuation and other clues in text can help students read smoothly and naturally. For example, a comma means to take a little pause. A period means to take a longer pause. An entire word in all caps means the reader should emphasize that word. A question mark means to ask the words as a question. An exclamation point tells a reader to read something a little faster and in an emotional tone appropriate to the context. Place a transparency of the top half of the Put Punctuation Here! reproducible (page 52) on an overhead projector. Read the passage without punctuation or inflection. Ask students if your reading sounded natural. Then, give each student a copy of the reproducible. Work with individual students to add appropriate punctuation, then reread the passage more naturally. Have students compare the two readings. To adjust for younger students, complete the activity as a whole class, including the comparison.

Put Punctuation Here!

Read the passage. Add the right punctuation so that you can read the paragraph naturally.

My name is Patricia I am starting the first grade this year I am so glad that I am not starting kindergarten I was so scared on my first day The school was very big and all of the people were bigger than me I wanted to go home with my mom but she said I would be just fine My teacher Mr Stewart who held the door open for me said that there would be a lot of toys in my classroom Everyone looked as scared as I was I learned to like kindergarten after I got used to all of the big people but it was much more fun to start first grade since I was not so small anymore

- -

Answer Key (answers may vary):

My name is Patricia. I am starting the first grade this year. I am so glad that I am not starting kindergarten! I was so scared on my first day. The school was very big, and all of the people were bigger than me. I wanted to go home with my mom, but she said I would be just fine. My teacher, Mr. Stewart, who held the door open for me, said that there would be a lot of toys in my classroom. Everyone looked as scared as I was. I learned to like kindergarten after I got used to all of the big people, but it was much more fun to start first grade since I was not so small anymore.

First-Rate Reading™: Fluency • CD-104016 • © Carson-Dellosa
Basics

Flow

Ahead of time, invite an adult volunteer to come to your classroom to read dialogue with you. Sit down with the volunteer before the lesson and write a conversation about a common topic. Perform this conversation for the class in two ways. Before reading, ask students to listen to the two different ways the same words are read. The first performance should be a choppy, word-by-word reading. The second performance should be a smooth and natural reading. Ask students which reading seemed more natural and why. Write their comments on the board. Explain that attributes students named help reading flow smoothly like a deep river, not be choppy like a raging river with many hills and rocks. Give each student a piece of white construction paper and instruct him to use a black crayon to write what makes a reader's words flow. (Students may copy the comments from the board.) Then, give each student watercolor paints and a paintbrush. Have him paint a gentle, flowing river over the crayon words and add other details, as well. Display the paintings on a bulletin board. Add the title "Our Words Flow like a River!"

Phrasing

Explain that reading in phrases helps a person sound natural. A smooth reader doesn't read a word, then stop, then read a word, then stop. A smooth reader reads groups of words at a time and then pauses. Write the following sentence on a sentence strip: *Before you cross the street, make sure you stop, look, and listen.* Read the sentence and stop after each word. Ask students if your reading sounded natural. Guide students to comment that it did not sound natural because you paused after each word instead of reading in phrases. Read the sentence again and ask students to listen for the pauses. Tell them that they will be harder to hear. Read the sentence naturally, such as, "Before you cross the street (slight pause), make sure you stop (slight pause), look (slight pause), and listen (stop)." Ask students to identify the pauses. Next, give each student a sentence strip. Write the following sentence on the board: *My mom said that we would get a new puppy, but I had to promise to help care for it!* Direct students to copy the sentence on their sentence strips. Then, have students read and reread the sentence until it sounds natural. Tell students to think about where the little pauses are. Direct students to cut their sentences into phrases while saying the words naturally. For example, "My mom said that we would get a new puppy," and "but I had to promise to help care for it!" Emphasize that when students practice reading, they should try to group words naturally. If some students are not reading at this level, pair skilled readers with less-skilled readers so that the skilled readers can help their partners hear the phrasing by modeling the reading.

All About Me! Autobiography

Have students write brief autobiographies to practice reading about subjects they know well—themselves! Distribute the All About Me! reproducible (page 55) to students. Direct them to complete the sentences on the sheet. Then, allow time for students to practice reading their autobiographies as naturally as possible with partners. Tell students that their reading should not sound choppy, but smooth, just like they are speaking to friends. When students feel ready, schedule time each day for a few students to read their autobiographies to the class. To help facilitate natural conversation, let students move their desks into a circle and read from their seats. After each reading, point out when the reader sounded natural and smooth.

Telephone Tag

Tell students that when they read, they should sound like they are having a conversation. Demonstrate with a conversation on the telephone. Before the assignment, record yourself having a brief conversation on the phone. Play it for students. Ask students to talk about whether you sounded similar to the way you sound when you are talking to the class. Next, assign students to pairs. Have each pair write a brief conversation they might have if they were speaking with each other on the telephone. Then, tell students to practice reading the dialogue until they sound natural. (If students are not ready to write dialogue, record each pair talking, then help the pair transcribe their conversation. Read it several times with students until they are familiar enough with it to practice on their own.) Give each pair two paper cups, a string, a sharpened pencil, and tape. Have the two create a "telephone." Each pair should use the pencil to poke holes through the bottoms of the cups, then thread one end of the string through the bottom of each cup. (Students will use opposite ends of the same string so that the cups are connected.) Use tape to secure the string to the insides of the cups. Allow time for students to practice reading their conversations while holding the telephone cups, then have students read their telephone conversations to the rest of the class. Record the conversations, if possible, and play them back to pairs so that they can evaluate how they sound.

Name _____

All About Me!

Finish each sentence about
yourself. Draw a picture of yourself in the frame.
Practice reading your answers naturally.

1. My name is _____.

2. I am _____ years old.

3. My favorite food is _____.

4. At recess, I like to _____.

5. My best day was when _____.

6. My favorite game is _____.

7. My favorite animal is _____.

8. I wish _____

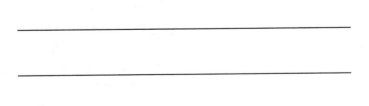

Conduct a Peer Interview

To help students practice making conversational reading, have them interview fellow students and read the interviews. Give each student a piece of paper and assign partners. At the top of the paper, have each student write *I am interviewing (partner's name)*. Tell students to think of five questions to ask their partners. If students cannot think of any questions, write these on the board for students to copy: *What's the nicest thing your sibling (or friend) ever did for you? If you could have any pet, what would it be? Why? What would you name it? Did you ever cut your own hair? What happened? If you could change your name, what would it be? Why? What is your favorite thing to do in school every day?* Next, have students write their questions, leaving enough space beneath each question to write the answer. When students have finished, have them switch papers. Direct partners to write their answers, then return the papers to the interviewers. Allow time for each interviewer and partner to practice reading the questions and responses. Then, have students switch roles. Explain that since students are reading things they wrote, the text should be familiar and sound like them, so they should be able to read smoothly.

Put On a Show

Bring out the "ham" in your students. Announce that students will be in a class theater troupe. Provide several books of children's plays with good dialogue, such as *Theatre for Young Audiences* edited by Coleman A. Jennings (St. Martin's Press, 1998). (As an alternative, have students choose familiar fairy tales and help them write plays without narrators.) Read the title of each play and the characters' names. Ask students to volunteer for different parts, or select the actors. Allow at least two weeks for students to practice reading their parts in a conversational tone. Explain that, to sound natural, as if they are really responding to each other, each student may change the way she reads her part slightly depending on how another student reads his. Remind students that they should not memorize their lines because that takes the focus away from reading. Schedule time for students to perform their plays. Invite other classes or parents to watch the plays.

What's on TV?

Ask students if they watched TV any night during the week. Call on a few students to share what they watched. Continue by asking if they would recommend the shows they watched and why. Point out that you are having a conversation about TV. The tone is natural. It flows very easily; there are no major gaps. Give each student a copy of the What's on TV? reproducible (page 57). Have each student think of his favorite TV show and write a paragraph about it on the reproducible. Suggest including a description, the reasons why he likes it, and if he would recommend watching it. If some students cannot generate enough text, prompt them with sentence starters to copy and fill in, such as *My favorite show is _____, I like it because _____, My favorite character on the show is _____ because _____,* etc. Have each student cut out the TV pattern on the reproducible. Allow time for students to practice reading their paragraphs smoothly and naturally. Pair students to read their paragraphs to each other. Walk around the room to hear different students read their work.

Name _____

What's on TV?

Describe your favorite TV show.
Why do you like it? Would you recommend it to a
friend? Write your response here.

Lunch Conversations

Help students practice flow in reading over lunch. Before lunch, tell students to think of topics they discuss with friends at lunchtime. During lunch, suggest that students listen to how the words and conversations sound. When students return, ask, "What topics did you discuss?" Write their answers on the board. Instruct each student to pick one subject listed and write a conversational paragraph about it. (For younger students, write a paragraph as a whole class.) After students have edited their paragraphs, give each student a paper plate. Tell students to copy their paragraphs onto the plates and to practice reading their paragraphs so that they sound natural and flow well. Then, set up the classroom to  resemble the lunchroom seating. Have students sit at "lunch" and take turns reading their paragraphs at least once to nearby classmates. While students are listening, allow them to eat snacks as a treat. (Before completing any food activity, ask parental permission and inquire about students' food allergies and religious or other food preferences.) Create a bulletin board with a checkered background by overlapping strips of red and white bulletin board paper to resemble a tablecloth. Staple the plates on top and add the title "Serving Up Smooth Reading."

Welcome, New Student!

Ask students if any of them have ever been the new student at school. Ask them what they felt like at first—maybe scared, nervous, afraid no one would like them, or excited and happy to be in a new place and meet new friends. Explain that it is difficult to be the new student at a school. New students don't know the routine or where anything is, and they often don't have friends yet. Have students write letters to a new student explaining how their classroom works. Remind students to keep the tone conversational and flowing. Give students pieces of paper and pencils. Start students off by writing *Dear New Student,* on the board. Depending on students' writing abilities, you may want to construct part or all of the letter as a whole class. When students are finished, have them practice reading their letters aloud at least four times so that they can check for mistakes and practice reading smoothly. Allow time for students to read their letters to the class. Collect the letters and put them together in a packet for the next new student in your classroom.

Calendar and Fluency

Incorporate fluency into daily routines. Choose three students to fluently read during an upcoming calendar time or morning message time. First, ask one student to write the day's menu in a conversational way. For example, the student may write *Today for lunch, the cafeteria is serving pizza, green beans, and a roll. For 20¢ more, you can buy an extra milk. Sound like a great meal!* Next, use a newspaper or the Internet to find the day's weather forecast. Then, have a student write a paragraph about the forecast in a natural, conversational tone. Ask a third student to write about the day's schedule and any special announcements, such as picture day or upcoming field trips. Allow all three students to practice reading their paragraphs the day before they plan to read aloud to the class. During calendar or morning message time, ask them to read their paragraphs to the class. Rotate so that every student gets to read part of the morning message at least once. If students are reluctant or very shy, pair them with other readers to read chorally.

Chapter Books

Encourage smooth reading by combining fluency practice with story time. Select a fun, grade-appropriate chapter book for the class to read aloud that has the same (or a greater) number of pages as the number of students in your class. Provide several copies of the same book. Preview the book with students, then assign one page to each student for the first two chapters. For the first chapter, select students who need less time to practice reading than others. Give books to both groups of students so that they can practice reading their pages aloud. Reinforce the idea of reading naturally and smoothly so that the audience will enjoy hearing the book. When the students reading chapter one seem ready, schedule time for each of them to read in front of the class, in the same order as the pages so that one chapter is covered. When the first chapter readers are done, select students for the third chapter as the second chapter readers finish preparing. At the beginning of each reading time, ask the previous day's readers to review what happened in their chapter so that the audience can remember the story. Continue to assign students two chapters ahead so that everyone gets enough practice before reading. (If some students need even more practice time, select their reading ahead of time from the end of the book. Assign them to practice at home with adults.) If there are more pages than students, ask for volunteers to practice and read other sections. When students have completed the book, provide a selection of similar books and let students vote on which book to read next.

Celebrity Scoop

Ask each student to choose a celebrity he would most like to be, such as an athlete, movie star, famous singer, etc. (Screen students' choices before completing the activity.) Pair students. Ask each student to picture the celebrity he will interview, write five questions he would like to ask that celebrity, then rejoin his partner. As the first interviewer asks questions, the "celebrity" should answer them as the real celebrity would answer them. The interviewer should write down the celebrity's answers. Then, have partners switch roles. When finished, tell students to rewrite their interviews as brief entertainment magazine articles. For example, if a student asks "Michael Jordan" the question, "How did you get started as a basketball player?" and the response was, "I used to play with my older brother, who won most of the games. I practiced a lot to get better and beat him," the interviewer would write the information in this manner: *Michael Jordan became a good basketball player by playing against his older brother. His brother won most of the time, so Michael practiced very hard to try to beat his brother.* Remind students that the tone of their articles should be very conversational because the information came from conversations and should be written as if they are going to be in a magazine. Younger students may need additional help changing from one format to another, and students who are not proficient at writing may need to dictate their questions and answers rather than writing them down. Let students practice reading their articles in a smooth, natural way. Then, schedule time for students to read their articles to the class. Remind the class that the information being read is probably not accurate because the "celebrities" are just pretending. When all students have read, combine the articles into a magazine. Add a cover and the title *Celebrity Scoop*.

Our Rules

Practice fluency with students, provide a gentle reminder of class rules, and communicate with parents at the same time. Review class rules with students. Ask students to elaborate on each rule by asking, "If you were telling a new classmate what this rule meant, what would you say?" Ask students for examples. Give each student a copy of the Our Rules reproducible (page 61). Tell students to explain the rules to their families. Have each student choose five rules and, on a separate piece of paper, write a few sentences about each rule. Encourage students to give examples of the rules, explain why they are important, or write about what the rules mean to them. You may need to model this several times in class. When they are finished, allow time for students to practice reading their explanations aloud several times. Listen to all students at least once so that you can correct any rule misunderstandings. Emphasize that students should sound natural when they read. Review what students wrote, send the rules home with students, and ask them to read the rules to their families. Ask families to sign the bottoms of the reproducibles indicating that they heard their children read the rules.

Name _____

Our Rules

Write five rules and explanations
below. Read them to your family and have
a parent or guardian sign the bottom of the sheet.

Dear Family,

We have been practicing reading in a natural, conversational way. Please allow time for your child to practice by reading our class rules. After you have heard the rules, please sign at the bottom of the sheet. Thank you!

Sincerely,

_____

Our Rules

1. _____
_____

2. _____
_____

3. _____
_____

4. _____
_____

5. _____
_____

_____ read the rules to me.
student's name

Parent's/Guardian's Signature _____

Personal History

Ask students to think about interesting things that happened to them in the previous grade. Let a few volunteers tell their stories. Next, ask students to think of experiences they had before the age of four. Students will find it much more difficult to recall stories from when they were this young without a little help. Give each student a copy of the Personal History reproducible (page 63). Have each student interview his family about his own personal history by asking family members to share stories about him when he was first born, one year old, two years old, three years old, and four years old. Suggest that each student listen to one story at a time, then write it in his own words on the reproducible. Have students interview their families that night and return the reproducibles the next day. Allow students to practice reading the stories to classmates or adults at least four times. Remind students that these stories came from conversations with their families, so when they read the responses aloud, they should sound conversational. Gather students into a large circle when it is time to read the stories. Tell each student to choose one story (or one age) to read to the class. Allow a few minutes for students to choose, then have each student read one piece of his personal history to the class.

What Did You Do at School Today?

It is an age-old problem. Families ask their children, "So, what did you do at school today?" The answer is usually some version of, "Nothing." Solve this problem by keeping parents informed while students practice fluency. Toward the end of the school day, review different events with students. Discuss topics studied, special classes (such as art or physical education), and lessons learned. Then, ask students to write brief letters to their families describing what happened. Consider modeling writing information about what happened at school. Remind students to keep the letters conversational, similar to how they talk to their families. Allow time for students to practice reading the letters before they leave for the day. Tell students to read the letters to their families. The next day, talk briefly with each student about whether she enjoyed the assignment, whether her letter was informative, whether her reading was smooth and natural, etc. If the assignment is successful, consider repeating it periodically and keep tabs on whether students' fluency improves for this particular assignment.

Reading Lesson

Ask students to think about what makes a reader sound natural. Is it the phrasing? The tone? Should the person sound like he is talking? Have students be teachers for a day by teaching younger students to read smoothly. Individually, in groups, or as a whole class, have students write directions for how to read a book smoothly. Have them use favorite books or chapters to give specific examples. Let students practice reading the selections and practice teaching lessons to classmates as well. Ask a teacher with younger students to let her class visit for a fluency lesson. Pair older and younger students. Have the older student give the lesson and demonstrate by reading, then be a listening partner for the younger student.

Name ______________________________

Naturalness, Smoothness, & Flow

Personal History

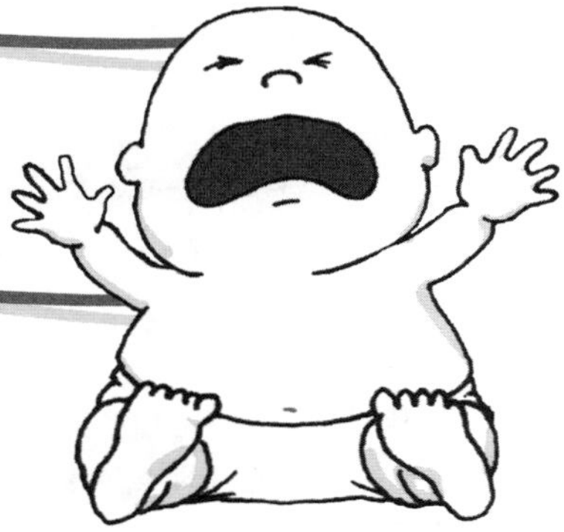

Dear Family,

We are writing about personal histories. Please allow time for your child to interview you about the first few years of his or her life. Thank you!

Sincerely,

____

1. When I was born, ____
____
____.

2. At one year old, ____
____
____.

3. When I was two years old, ______________________________________
____
____.

4. At three years old, ____
____
____.

5. When I was four years old, ______________________________________
____
____.

Pen Pals

A pen pal gives each student a purpose for writing a conversational letter. Reading that letter aloud allows the student to check for correct tone and punctuation clues. Partner with another class to set up a pen pal network. When you have selected pen pals, write their names on slips of paper for students to draw, or consider pairing students by ability or common interests. Give each student a copy of the Pen Pals reproducible (page 65). Tell each student to write a conversational letter to his pen pal on the reproducible. The letters should sound like students are talking to their pen pals. (Students will get a better feel for this as they get to know their pen pals through writing.) Allow students to practice reading their letters aloud with partners or small groups. Then, have pairs of students read the letters and give feedback by answering these questions: "Did the letter sound like a conversation? Was it natural and smooth? Which parts worked well and why?" Give students time to revise (if they want to revise) and send their letters. Hopefully, you'll get quite a few responses! If you and the other teacher are both interested in promoting fluency with this activity, let students record their letters on a cassette tape. Have each student tell whom his letter is for so that the recipient knows when to listen. Send the tape with a list of writers' and recipients' names in the order that they appear on the tape so that the other teacher can call students to the listening center in the right order. When the pen pals respond, ask their teacher to have them give brief feedback about fluency.

Next Year

Ask students to think about how they felt at the end of the previous year. Were they nervous or excited about what the next grade would be like? Many students share these feelings at the end of the year. Explain that you want younger students to feel at ease about moving to this grade level. Have students create an audio journal to help younger students. Allow students to group themselves by interest areas. Each group should answer one of these questions: "What do you learn in math? What kinds of books do you read? What is social studies like? What experiments do you do in science? What are music, art, and P.E. (physical education) like? Where do you sit in the cafeteria (or other lunch-related question)? Is there much homework (or other homework-related question)?" Instruct each group to write a script that tells about their question. Tell students to make sure that the script includes which member reads each answer. Allow time for the groups to read their scripts. Visit each group during practice time to consult with them on fluency, and focus on whether they sound smooth and natural. Explain that since they will be trying to set younger students at ease, they should sound relaxed and conversational when talking. Finally, let each group record a reading. Arrange for younger students to visit, preferably those who may be assigned to your class next year. Before the meeting, let groups make signs that designate their subject areas. Play the recording for the younger students. After each script, let the younger students ask related questions from that group, and record the question-and-answer sessions if possible. Repeat with all groups. When the visitors leave, if time permits, play some of the script recordings and the subsequent question-and-answer sessions, and compare them. Is one more fluent than the other? Why? You may want to save the recordings for the first school day next year. It will be a great way to transition new students to your classroom!

Name _____

Pen Pals

Wrenn Richards
Mr. Pinelli's Class
Kennedy School
Room 105

DENVER, CO 133
PM
31 MAY
2003

Eric Davis
Mrs. Smithson's Class
Kennedy School
Room 28

Write a letter to your pen pal. Make the words sound like you are talking to the person.

Dear Pen Pal,

My name is _____ . I have ____ brothers and

sisters. I am _____ years old. How old are you?

My favorite thing to do is _____

_____ .

The first time I did my favorite thing was when _____

_____ .

What do you like to do? My favorite part of school is _____

because _____

_____ .

What is your favorite part? I wish that _____ .

_____ .

If you could wish for anything, what would it be? Write back soon!

Sincerely,

_____
(your name)

Performance

Introduction

Performing is a great way for students to practice fluency skills. Students feel like they have a reason to practice their reading because there is an end goal. It is also different from more traditional methods for teaching language arts. Students have fun acting, moving around, working with classmates, and being creative. Parents also enjoy watching their young readers perform in front of an audience. Use the activities to culminate your fluency work and to reward students for their progress.

Readers' Theater

When performing readers' theater, students follow along on a script while some students read individual parts. It is very much like a play, except there is no expectation for students to memorize the script—the point is to read directly from it. Also, there are usually no sets or costumes in readers' theater. (Although, you may certainly add those.) Typically, students sit or stand together on a "stage" (or even at their desks), wearing their regular school clothes. Readers' theater is a wonderful way to get students to read a text multiple times. Their goal is to be ready to perform the readers' theater in a given amount of time. Any rehearsals are really just opportunities for students to reread the script. Readers' theater also helps students practice all of the fluency skills together. Performers must be accurate, automatic, expressive, and natural, or they won't sound convincing in front of their audience. Plan to do some readers' theater with your class. There are several Web sites that offer free readers' theater scripts, which are easily found by doing a search for readers' theater scripts. Other resources for readers' theater are teachers' books like *Frantic Frogs and Other Frankly Fractured Folktales for Readers' Theater* by Anthony D. Fredericks (Libraries Unlimited, 1993) and *Readers' Theater for Beginning Readers* by Suzanne I. Barchers (Libraries Unlimited, 1993).

The Great Debate

Explain that a debate is an event in which two people or groups advocate opposite sides of an issue. Often in a debate, the two people prepare their speeches ahead of time, and must read them fluently and eloquently in order to win. Sometimes debaters are assigned to speak in favor of topics that, in real life, they do not support. Debating the other side of an issue forces them to be knowledgeable about both sides of an argument. With students, brainstorm several appropriate topics for them to debate, such as the pros and cons of school uniforms, cafeteria food selections, amounts of homework, field trips (to go or not to go), etc. Write topic suggestions on the board until there is one topic for every two students. Assign each topic to a pair. Direct each student to write a one-minute speech either for or against the topic, and insist that students in the same pair take opposing sides. Have students practice reading their speeches. Since the debates are so short, schedule several debates a day.

Film Festival

Explain that film festivals around the world show new films or sometimes showcase older films with something in common (same subject, same director, etc.). Have each student write, produce, illustrate, and direct her own animated film based on a life experience. Give each student a Film Festival Planner reproducible (page 68). First, ask each student to write a story about a funny or interesting thing that happened to her. The basic facts must be true, but students may embellish the details a bit. Discuss each student's topic before moving ahead in the lesson. After each student writes the story on her reproducible, have her list the characters and setting. Explain that each story must have a beginning, middle, and end. Have each student underline the beginning of her story with a blue crayon, underline the middle with a yellow crayon, and underline the end with a red crayon. If a student finds that she does not have enough detail in one section, encourage her to rewrite the story on another piece of paper. Next, instruct each student to write the beginning, middle, and end on separate sheets of paper. Then, have each student turn over the pages and illustrate those parts of the story on the backs. Let students practice reading their stories with accuracy and expression. For the Film Festival, have students hold up the picture sides to the audience as they fluently read the stories aloud. Remind students to use different voices for different characters.

Science Show

Cross-curricular activities are good for practicing fluency because they can take some of the focus (and some of the pressure) off of reading aloud. Provide an assortment of grade-appropriate science experiments that require few supplies and can be performed in a short amount of time, and lead students to put on a science performance. Give each student time to look through the selection and choose a simple science experiment he would like to demonstrate. After students have cleared their selections with you, have students rewrite the experiments in their own words. To keep the audience's interest, remind students that they must be accurate, expressive, automatic, and natural as they present. Remind students that the text should sound like they usually talk because they are performing it. Have students practice reading the directions until they feel fluent. Then, encourage them to practice with their experiment materials so that they know what to expect on performance day. When students are ready, schedule a few science performances a day. If possible, videotape the performances. Play the science show tape to the class when all of the experiments are completed, or during a school science fair, parents' night, or open house.

Film Festival Planner

Use this planning sheet to prepare
for your film.

1. Tell a funny story that happened to you.

   _____

   _____

   _____

   _____

   _____

   _____

2. List the characters in your story.

   _____

   _____

   _____

3. What is the setting for your story?

   _____

   _____

   _____

4. Underline the beginning of your story with a blue crayon.
5. Underline the middle of your story with a yellow crayon.
6. Underline the end of your story with a red crayon.
7. Rewrite the beginning, middle, and end on three pieces of paper.
8. Draw the beginning, middle, and end of your story on the backs of your revisions.

First-Rate Reading™: Fluency • CD-104016 • © Carson-Dellosa
Basics

Tools of the Trade

Get students involved with open house or parents' night and promote fluency at the same time. Tell students that when their families come to school, they like to see what students are learning. Write the words *reading, math, science,* and *social studies* on the board. Ask students to think of tools they use to learn about each subject. For example, books and posters can teach about reading; manipulatives, calculators, and rulers can help with math; maps and timelines are used for social studies, microscopes and beakers are used for science, etc. After the brainstorming session, give each student a copy of the Tools of the Trade reproducible (page 70). Have students explain these tools to their families. Let each student choose a school tool. Direct each student to write a brief paragraph that describes the tool, names the subject for which the tool is used, and explains how students use the tool in the classroom. Allow time for students to practice reading their paragraphs with accuracy, automaticity, expression, and smoothness. On open house night or parents' night, station students at different points around the classroom, perhaps near the subject areas' centers, to explain their tools as families browse. If students cannot participate in one of these events, videotape students, create a sign-up sheet, and let students take home the videotape for their families to see.

Class Talent Show

Every teacher knows that students have talent. Let students showcase their talents and practice fluency at the same time by holding a class talent show. Have each student choose a talent that is appropriate to perform at school, such as playing an instrument, doing magic tricks, reading a book aloud, drawing a picture, telling jokes, doing a dance, singing a song, doing a cartwheel, dribbling a basketball, etc. After you have approved the list of talents, have each student write an introductory paragraph describing his talent. Direct each student to include a description about where he learned it and what he will show. Students should practice reading their introductions several times. Then, have students practice reading their introductions and performing their talents. Schedule time for the talent show. Invite families or other guests to attend this fabulous showcase of talent!

Tools of the Trade

Choose a "school tool." Write about
it here. Read your writing aloud.

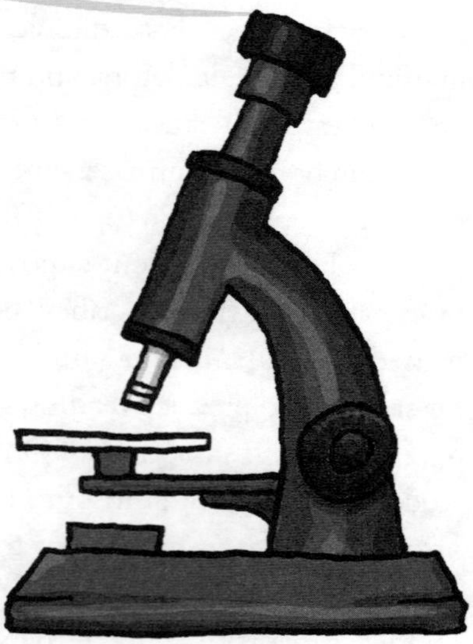

My tool is _____

_____

_____

We use this tool in _____

(school subject)

This is how we use it: _____

_____

_____

_____

_____

_____

_____

_____

_____

_____

_____

First-Rate Reading™: Fluency • CD-104016 • © Carson-Dellosa
Basics

Birthday Poems

Provide a book that has birthday poems, such as *Birthday Rhymes, Special Times* by Bobbye S. Goldstein (Doubleday, 1993). Share several poems aloud and let students vote on their favorite. Write the poem and its title on a piece of chart paper. Have students practice reading the special birthday poem. First, have students follow along while you read the poem aloud with expression and accuracy. Then, direct students to read the poem aloud with you three times. Finally, tell students to read the poem without your help. When a student is celebrating a birthday, have her classmates read the poem to her chorally. Periodically, use other popular poems to further challenge students.

Oh, Say Can You Sing?

Collaborate with the school music teacher to teach students fluency. Ask the music teacher to share song lyrics students are currently working with so that students can practice them in your classroom. Give each student a copy of the lyrics to read through several times while you familiarize yourself with them. Remind students that musical performers sing accurately, automatically, and expressively. Ask students to imagine what songs would sound like if singers stopped to sound out words! Read a song aloud to the class, then have students read the song with you. Next, have students read the song by themselves. Finally, schedule a reading and singing session with the music teacher. Before the session, ask her to comment on students' improved fluency.

Parade of Presidents

Incorporate social studies into fluency lessons. Introduce students to past US Presidents. (Adjust this activity as needed for prime ministers or other country leaders.) Explain that while students may be familiar with more famous Presidents, there are also less famous Presidents. Tell students that there have been over 40 Presidents of the United States. Help students find the names of all Presidents. Assign each student one President about which to research interesting facts and stories. (To avoid currently controversial topics, use the first 30 Presidents.) Then, tell students to write one or two paragraphs about their Presidents in first person so that it sounds like their Presidents are speaking. Allow students to practice reading their paragraphs expressively, accurately, smoothly, and in "presidential voices." Schedule a day for the Parade of Presidents. Have students present their Presidents in chronological order. Consider allowing students to wear costumes as they give their performances. If students enjoy the activity, repeat with First Ladies, explorers, inventors, etc.

A Story of Toys

Ask each student to choose his favorite toy. Instruct each student to write a paragraph describing the toy—where it comes from, what it does, how long he has owned it, and why it is his favorite. Then, give each student a copy of the Story of Toys Rubric reproducible (page 73). Explain that a rubric is a way to judge how well a student can perform a particular skill. Also, let students know that they will read their stories aloud to the class. Tell them that you will use the rubric to assess their performances, so they should keep these skills in mind as they practice. Review the rubric with the class. (See previous chapters for a detailed description of each skill.) Then, have each student read his paragraph aloud several times. After students have had a chance to practice reading their "toy stories," invite them to bring in their toys and read their writing to the class. Fill out a Story of Toys Rubric reproducible after watching each performance.

Best in Show

Create a fluency assignment for the animal lovers in your classroom. Provide white bulletin board paper, crayons, and scissors for each student. Also, provide a book or another resource that describes various dog breeds. (The Internet is a great source for dog breed information.) Explain that there are many different breeds and show examples. Tell students that different breeds have different character traits. Some of them like to chase rodents, others like to herd cows and sheep, still others can find lost people just from scents. Allow each student to choose and research a different dog breed. Encourage students to find out what they look like (including size), what their typical personalities are, and whether they are used for any particular jobs. Have each student write one or two paragraphs describing her dog breed, then give students plenty of time to practice reading their paragraphs. On the bulletin board paper, direct each student to draw a life-sized picture of her dog (assist with measurements if necessary), color it, and cut it out. Schedule time for your class "dog show." Ask students to show their dogs and read their paragraphs. (They may need classmates to hold up the pictures while they read.) After everyone has presented, collect the paragraphs and pictures. Use the hallway bulletin board or a large wall to create a display. Staple the dog pictures and paragraphs next to each other. Add the title "Best in Show."

Story of Toys Rubric

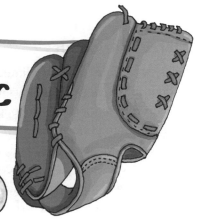

Listen to each student read out loud.
Rate each skill listed below by circling a number
from 1–5. The worst score is 1 and the best is 5.

Student's Name _____

Date _____   Topic _____

Fluency Skills

1. Accuracy   1   2   3   4   5
   (needs practice)   (getting better)   (very good)

2. Automaticity   1   2   3   4   5
   (needs practice)   (getting better)   (very good)

3. Expressiveness   1   2   3   4   5
   (needs practice)   (getting better)   (very good)

4. Flow   1   2   3   4   5
   (needs practice)   (getting better)   (very good)

Total Score for Performance: _____

Comments: _____

_____

_____

_____

Merry Marionettes

Select a few fairy tales or folktales that could be easily rewritten as plays and that have enough parts for each student in the class. If students are familiar with the stories, they may be able to write the plays from memory. Explain that marionettes are puppets whose arms and legs are moved with strings. Have students create marionettes to perform the stories. Assign one group to each story, and assign a student to each part (including a narrator). Have group members work together to write a story into a play so that it includes dialogue. Have each group select a "secretary" (someone with nice handwriting who can write quickly). The secretary should write the play by writing each character's name, a colon, and then the dialogue. For example, a secretary writing about the *Three Little Pigs* might write, *Straw House Pig: Not by the hair of my chinny chin chin.* Make an additional copy of the completed play for each group member. Encourage students to highlight or underline their lines, and give groups ample time to practice reading their parts. Remind students that their reading should be accurate and expressive because the marionettes will not be able to show their emotions through facial expressions.

Next, give students instructions for how to make marionettes. Give each student a copy of the Merry Marionettes reproducible (page 76), two craft sticks or rulers, light-colored thread, black yarn, scissors, crayons or markers, tagboard or construction paper, glue, clear tape, masking tape, and a hole puncher. Tell students to follow the steps below as you read them and model the process. Explain that there are front and back pieces for each body part on the reproducible. Note that younger children will need more assistance, so let adult volunteers help them with building the marionettes.

1. Let students appropriately color the pieces on the reproducible to match their characters and cut them out. (Body parts are labeled on the reproducible.)

2. Have each student cut five pieces of black yarn for the arms, legs, and neck. The four arm and leg pieces should each be about 2" (5 cm) long, and the neck piece should be about 1" (2.5 cm) long.

3. Work with one set, or "side" of the pieces first. Have each student place these pieces decorated side down in the following order: a head piece at the top, a body piece in the middle, two hand pieces to either side of the body piece, and two foot pieces below the body. Have each student make a neck by gluing or taping the small piece of yarn to connect the head and body. Then, have each student glue the arm yarn onto the hands and body, and glue the leg yarn from the feet to the body.

4. Instruct students to make a "sandwich" by gluing or taping the matching body parts (decorated side up) on top of the existing body parts and yarn. The sandwich should be a body part, yarn, and then the matching body part on top. Have students hold the pieces in place for a few seconds until the glue dries. (The paper may curl if it is not held down for at least 30 seconds.)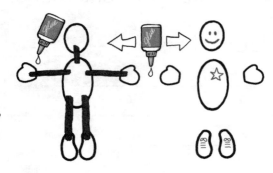

5. Have each student glue or rubber-band two craft sticks together as shown.

6. Direct each student to cut five pieces of thread, approximately 12" (30 cm) in length. Tie one piece of thread to the marionette's "wrist." Wrap the other end of thread around one end of a craft stick and take up the slack until the arm is hanging slightly. Secure the thread with masking tape. Repeat with the other arm and both feet.

7. Have each student put a piece of clear tape over the head to reinforce the paper and punch a hole in the head through the tape. Tie the thread through the hole. Wrap the other end of the thread around the center of the craft sticks, and take up the slack so that the head is higher than the arms. Secure with masking tape.

8. Let each student use tagboard or construction paper to add other details, including ears, a tail, clothing, or anything that is appropriate for the character.

9. Have students practice moving their marionettes by trying to make them wave their arms and legs, walk, and fall on the ground.

Just before the performance, turn a table on its side to be the stage. Hang a sheet or curtain over the table so that the bottom of the sheet is the same height as the top of the table. Have students stand behind the table and curtain and extend their arms into the space behind the curtain to operate the marionettes in front of the table. (The curtain will block students from view while their marionettes will move in front of the table.) Allow time for students to practice reading their scripts while moving their marionettes. Set up a time for the performances. Invite guests to attend the show.

Merry Marionettes

Cut apart the pieces.
Glue them together to make a marionette.

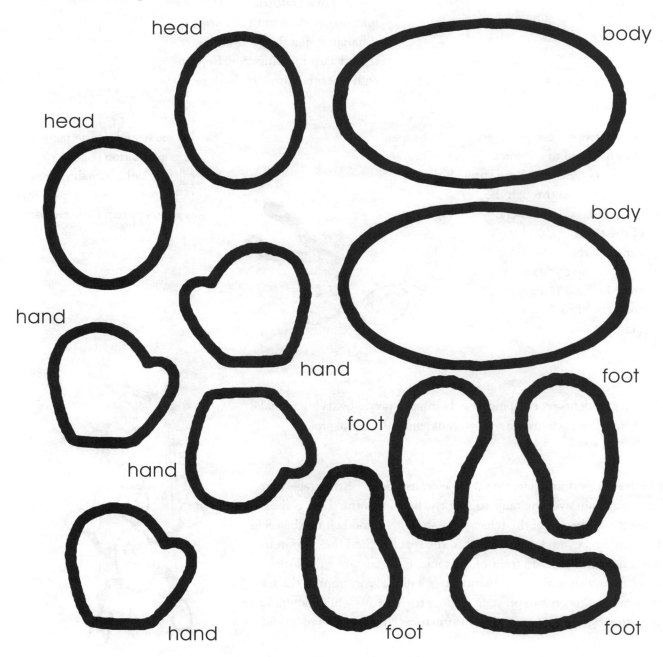

head   body

head

body

hand   hand   foot

foot

hand   foot   foot

First-Rate Reading™: Fluency • CD-104016 • © Carson-Dellosa
Basics

Groovy Poetry Party

Poetry is a great way to practice fluency. The text is typically short and fun to read, and has a rhythm to it that helps move students' reading along smoothly. Motivate students to read by having a Groovy Poetry Party. Provide poetry books and have each student choose a favorite poem. Or, focus the poem selection on a theme such as the current season. Give students time to practice reading their poems. Remind students to read with accuracy, automaticity, expression, and smoothness. When students are ready to recite, organize a Groovy Poetry Party. Work with students to make invitations for their parents. Encourage everyone to wear a 1960's-inspired costume. After the guests arrive, have students read their poems in front of the audience. As a show of approval, ask the audience to snap their fingers instead of clapping. Groovy, man!

Author! Author!

Pay tribute to beloved authors while practicing fluency at the same time. Ask each student to choose an author she has read during the past few months and conduct research on the author. (Most children's authors have terrific Web sites.) Have her write a brief paragraph in first person talking about the author's life, his books and illustrations (if the author also illustrates), and more specifically about one book he has written. Help each student obtain a copy of her favorite book and practice reading a short passage from it, as well as her paragraph, until she can read both texts fluently. On author day, ask each student to bring in simple props to identify herself as that author. For example, a student performing as Eric Carle could wear glasses and a cotton beard and bring in a toy caterpillar. Let each "author" stand in front of the class with her props, read her autobiographical paragraph, and then share a reading from the chosen book.

Tour Guide

Tell students that they will be tour guides. Explain that a tour guide may show a traveler the best part of a country and tell interesting facts about it. Give each student a copy of the Tour Guide reproducible (page 78). Assign a country to each student. Have students research their countries and fill in the information on the reproducibles. After students have found and recorded the information, have them write it in their own words on different pieces of paper. You may designate the form you would like for them to use. Give students time to practice reading the information fluently and encourage each student to create a visual aid, such as a poster, brochure, "photo" album, or small billboard, to show the highlights of the country. Schedule time for the "tour guides" to give their presentations. You may want to designate this day as "travel day" and ask students to wear travel clothes (safari clothes, Hawaiian print shirts, etc.).

Name _____

Tour Guide

Research a country. Draw a
picture of the flag and write the name of the
language. Use your research to help you write a
paragraph about that country.

My country is _____.

The flag looks like this:

_____ is the primary language spoken in this country.

When you visit, this is what you will see: _____

_____

_____

_____

_____

_____

_____

_____

_____

Mix and Match

Promote fluency with a silly game. Tell each student to choose a favorite picture book. (Older students may choose chapters from chapter books.) Give students ample time to practice reading the books fluently. Remind students to be accurate (make few mistakes), automatic (learn the words ahead of time so that they recognize them instantly), expressive (think about what the characters are thinking and feeling), and smooth (read by phrases, instead of word-by-word). When students can read their selections perfectly, have them record their readings on audiocassettes. (Teach students how to use the tape recorder, tape them yourself, or ask an adult volunteer to record the readings.) Next, have each student pretend to read a new book by mouthing the words while the tape-recorded sound of someone else's voice is playing. (It will look like Ella's voice is coming out of Omar's mouth.) Pair students who are at approximately the same reading level. Have the pairs switch books and practice reading the new books fluently. (Even though the audience will not hear the new person reading, each student will still have to practice so that she can follow along with someone else's reading.) Give each student time to practice mouthing the words while listening to her partner's voice on tape. (Use donated, handheld cassette players with headphones or let students use the listening center individually.) Consider allowing each pair to practice both books chorally. When students are ready, play one tape and have the partner "read" the story to the class by mouthing the words while her partner's voice is reading the book. Students have now practiced fluency twice!

Fluent Flo

Give each student a copy of the Fluent Flo reproducible (page 80) and a paper bag. Explain that the reproducible shows how to make Fluent Flo. Tell students that Fluent Flo knows the different fluency skills, and she knows that the more she practices, the more fluent she will be. Direct students' attention to the large rectangle on the reproducible. Explain that there are four aspects of being a fluent reader: accuracy, automaticity, expressiveness, and smoothness. Help students write a definition for each aspect. Next, direct students to cut along the outsides of the face shapes. Tell each student to turn his bag upside down and glue the large rectangle on the back of the paper bag. Next, instruct students to glue the faces to the other sides of the bags. Allow each student to add yarn hair on top of the bag above the eyes. Have each student fold the bag where she has glued the mouth, put her hand inside the bag, and practice moving Flo's head as if she is talking. Direct each student to read and reread the definitions that are written on Flo's back. Assign students to groups of four. Let each group member use Flo to read one of the definitions on the back. Each student should move Flo's mouth as she reads the definition. At the end of the lesson, review the definition for each skill.

Fluent Flo

Write a definition for each part of fluency. Cut out the pieces and glue them to a paper bag to make Fluent Flo.

Fluent Reading is:

1. Accurate.

   Definition: _____

   _____

2. Automatic.

   Definition: _____

   _____

3. Expressive.

   Definition: _____

   _____

4. Smooth.

   Definition: _____

   _____

Remember, the best way to become a fluent reader is to practice, practice, practice.

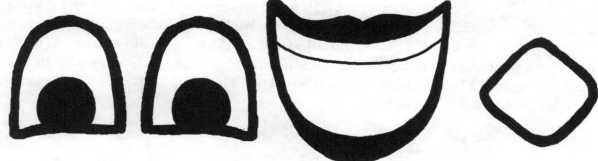

First-Rate Reading™: Fluency • CD-104016 • © Carson-Dellosa
Basics